Cast Iron Cooking

Easy Cast Iron Skillet
Home Cooking Recipes

Marie Adams

ISBN: 978-1544139111

Printed in the United States

Contents

Before we Begin… 1

Get to Know Cast Iron Cookware 3

Seasoning 4

Maintenance 5

Health Benefits 6

Cast Iron Cooking Tips 7

Recipes 9

Breakfast Recipes 9

Breezy Brunch Skillet 9

Steak and Eggs Benedict 11

Sunny Skillet Breakfast 13

Farm House Breakfast 15

Spicy Potato Hash Browns 17

Caprese Skillet Eggs 19

Berry Pancakes 21

Breakfast Scramble 23

Main Dishes/Entree Recipes 25

Poultry 25

Chicken and Dressings 25

Spinach Stuffed Sundried Tomato Chicken 27

Roasted Rosemary Chicken 29

Chicken Pot Pie 31

Dijon and Wine Roasted Chicken 33

Sage Roasted Chicken with Rustic Vegetables 35

Spicy Chicken and Lemongrass Peanut Noodles 36

Basil Balsamic Baked Chicken 37

Old World Chicken Parmesan 39

Kung Pao Chicken 41

Crispy Coconut Chicken Tenders 42

Lemon Garlic Dipping Sauce 43

Honey Garlic Chicken Thighs with Broccoli Slaw 44

Orange Ginger Chicken 45

Sausage-and-Chicken Cassoulet 47

Baked Asiago Chicken and Mushroom Pasta...................49
Buffalo Chicken and Ranch Rice 50
Cornish Game Hen with Bacon and Onions 51
Ranch Chicken Mac and Cheese 53
Creamy Chicken Enchilada Skillet....................................55
Succulent Madras Chicken Curry 57
Louisiana BBQ Dipping Sauce...58
Chicken Pot Pie Pastry 59
Turkey Pot Pie 61
Cast Iron Turkey Burgers 63
Chicken Biryani with Mint Chutney..................................65
Chicken Jambalaya 67
Chicken Thighs on Artichoke Heart..................................68
Cashew-Parm Chicken...69
Chicken with Spinach and Raspberry Stuffing.................70
Chicken with Asparagus Bacon Bundles..........................71
Healthy BBQ Chicken Pizza..72
Beef 73
Tri Colored Stuffed Pepper Casserole...............................73
Skillet Lasagna 75
Cast Iron Cheeseburgers...77
Mexican Skillet Casserole...79
Beef and Potato Pie..81
Beef Stroganoff 83
Greek Beef Stew 86
Beef and Rosemary Dumplings 87
Mole Chile and Cornbread 89
Italian Beef and Tomatoes 91
Spaghetti and Meatballs 92
Deep Dish Beef Lovers Pizza 93
Orange Ginger Beef on Egg Noodle Bed...........................95
Simply Delicious Beef Chili 96
Delicious Pan Quesadillas...97
Rich Heritage Lasagna...99
All in One Hamburger Casserole 101
Green Chile Tamale Pie.. 103

Cast Iron Roast Beef 105

Creamy Basil Flank Steak 107

The Best Beef Sliders 109

Korean Spiced Beef and Jasmine Rice 110

Mexicasa Beef Tacos 111

Red Beef Curry 112

Pancetta Meatballs with Red Bell Slaw 113

Beef Ragu 114

Beef and Sweet Potato Casserole 115

Succulent Steak Salad with Sweet Potato 116

Mini Eggplant Lasagna 117

Pork and Lamb 119

Creamed Corn and Bacon Skillet 119

Pork Chops with Pepper Jelly Sauce 121

Cider Baked Pork and Apple 123

Bright and Early Sausage Potato Hash 125

Big Ranch Chops and Vegetables 127

Grilled Pork Quesadillas 128

Pancetta Scallion Creamy Mac and Cheese 129

Chorizo Tamale Pie 131

Mushroom Pork Chops 133

Cinnamon Scented Pork Medallions 135

Easy Sweet Pea and Pork Casserole 137

Cherry-Glaze Pork Chops and Green Beans 138

Italian Sausage Baked Spaghetti 139

Lamb Kabobs with Shepherd's Salad 141

New York Sausage and Peppers Sandwich 143

Pork and Broccoli Skillet 144

BBQ Pork Chops 145

Pork Loin with Sweet Potato 146

Lamb and Butternut Squash Stew 147

Middle Eastern Spiced Lamb 148

Fish and Seafood 149

Shrimp Piccata 149

Shrimp and Chorizo Paella 150

White Wine Braised Salmon and Baked Potatoes 151

Cajun Shrimp Alfredo.. 152

Pecan Fried Catfish 153

Oyster Brunch 155

Dill Butter Salmon and Rice 157

Pineapple Shrimp Stir Fry.. 158

Shrimp Jambalaya.. 159

Smokey Bacon and Crab Chowder................................... 161

Sweet and Spicy Scallops 163

Spicy Lemon Whitefish 164

Orange Cranberry Tilapia Salad 165

Wild Salmon with Yellow Squash 166

Prosciutto-Wrapped Cod Filet and Zucchini 167

Fish Tacos with Orange Cilantro Salad 168

Garlic Shrimp in Mushroom Vestibules............................ 169

Shrimp and Sausage Gumbo 170

Vegetarian and Side.. 171

Root Vegetable Pot Pie 171

Creamy Green Vegetable Skillet Pasta 173

Buttermilk Cornbread... 175

Ooey-Gooey Mac'n Cheese 176

Bok Choy Chinese Noodles... 177

Lemony Wild Mushroom and Broccoli Pasta.................... 178

Zesty Eggplant Parmesan.. 179

Sweet Potato Burrito Skillet 181

White Bean and Southern Greens Chili............................. 183

Crisp Green Bean and Egg Hash 184

Rosemary Sweet Potato Side 185

Italian Bean and Tomato Casserole 186

Pasta and Greens Torte 187

Potato and Onion Flatbread 189

Mediterranean Quiche.. 191

Greek Linguine 192

Hot and Crispy Vegetable Salad 193

Cauliflower and Sweet Potato Curry................................. 194

Garlic Asparagus Sauté 195

Veggie Lasagna 196

Creamy Zucchini Slides.. 197

ZuCa Noodles 198

Cauliflower Flecked with Basil and Pine Nut 199

Flaxseed Tortilla 200

Soups... 201

Ham and Double Cheese Soup 201

Bacon Potato Winter Soup 202

Portobello Porcini Mushroom Soup 203

Hearty White Bean and Turkey Soup 204

Grandma's Chicken Noodle Soup 205

Pork and Cabbage Soup... 206

Parmesan Chicken Soup 207

Smooth Lentil Carrot Soup.. 208

Shitake Chicken Soup 209

Steak and Broccoli Soup 210

Desserts 211

Blueberry Peach Pie 211

Lemon Poppy seed Dump Cake.................................... 213

Cherry Clafouti 214

Caramel Apple Cake 215

Peach Tart.. 217

Maple Vanilla Custard 219

Fruit N Cream Crêpes 220

Cookie in a Pan 221

Raspberry White Chocolate Dump Cake........................ 223

Apple Caramel Cake 224

Apple Pie... 225

Chocolate Chip Dutch Baby 227

Mini Berry Cobbler 229

Cinnamon Raisin Nut Dump Cake 231

Walnut Apple Crumble.. 232

Conclusion 233

More Books by Marie Adams... 235

Appendix – Cooking Conversion Charts 237

Before we Begin...

Cast iron cooking has been a common culinary method for centuries, yet in modern times many of us shy away from using cast iron, or may even be intimidated by it. Cast iron cooking is rich in history, but also rich in myths that it is difficult and temperamental to work with. The truth is that cast iron is not only easy to use, its durability means that the little bit of effort that you put into it will pay you back tenfold in over its lifetime of use.

Cast iron cookware is great because of its versatility. It allows you to cook meals in one simple piece of cookware that would normally require all sorts of pots and pans. You can easily use cast iron on the stovetop for sautéing, stir-fry's, and soups, or use it in the oven, or both. Using cast iron for Paleo is particularly helpful since you can cook your proteins and veggies, from stovetop to oven, all in one dish.

Snuggling up to a cozy bowl of soup or a luscious casserole on a cool winter's eve is just one of those magical things that make the chilly weather a welcome visitor. Not only are these kinds of comfort dishes delicious, they are also supremely easy to make thanks to the magic of cast iron cookware.

The cast iron cooked evenly and was a breeze to clean, even when the meal was a messy recipe.

Although cast iron cookware has been around for several hundred years, its popularity has made a resurgence as more and more cooks of the new age are embracing the ease of this traditional cookware and incorporating it into their busy lives.

The versatility of cast iron cookware has given it its staying power. With our busy lives, the beauty of a one-pot dish designed to keep everyone happy is a welcome reprieve for any cook. They are sure to be hit even with the pickiest eaters, and only you need to know how easy it was!

Happy cooking,

Get to Know Cast Iron Cookware

Before we get into all the different recipes that you can use with the cast iron skillet, it is important to take the time to understand your cast iron skillet. Not using it properly can destroy your skillet quickly, but with proper care, cast iron can last for decades.

This chapter will cover everything you need to know about getting your cast iron skillet read and keeping it perfect.

When and where were cast iron cookware invented?

While we often think of cast iron as something fairly new, it has actually been around since the 5th century BC. In fact, cast iron artefacts have been discovered from Ancient China, where it is believed to have been invented.

Originally used to make ploughshares, the Ancient Chinese also used it to make pots and even weapons. However, despite how old cast iron is, it did not come to Europe until the 15th century AD. During this time, cast iron was used for cannons.

In the 1700's, a man by the name of Abraham Darby began creating pots and kettles from cast iron when he found a way to produce the pots with a thinner amount of iron. It was through this process that owning cast iron became a popular choice, and cast iron cookware has been found in homes ever since.

Seasoning

Although you may be able to purchase cast iron with a non-stick surface, the majority of cast iron skillets, saucepan and Dutch oven are not sold like that. Actually, I recommend getting an untreated cast iron skillet so that you can season it yourself.

While the term seasoning brings to mind adding spices, seasoning actually means **making a cast iron cookware non-stick. This should be done before you use your cast iron cookware for the first time and any time your skillet begins to look dull.**

To season your cast iron skillet, follow the steps below:

1. Preheat the oven to 350°F.

2. Wash the new skillet. This can be done with warm, soapy water, and a sponge. Do not use steel wool as you can scratch the pan and ruin it. Wash it thoroughly. It should be noted that this is the only time you use soapy water when cleaning the cast iron. After it is seasoned, do not use soap.

3. Rinse the skillet, and make sure that it is completely free of soap.

4. Dip a paper towel in vegetable oil.

5. Rub the oiled paper towel over the cast iron skillet. You should cover both the inside and outside of the cast iron skillet. Make sure it is a thick, even coat on the skillet.

6. Place in the preheated oven. Make sure the skillet is upside down and in the center of the oven. To catch oil drips, put a baking sheet or aluminum foil under it.

7. Bake the cast iron skillet for an hour. Do not remove it sooner than an hour or the seasoning process won't be perfect.

8. Turn off the oven, but leave the cast iron skillet in the oven.

9. Allow it to cool completely. Cast iron holds heat for a long time so it may take several hours to cool.

10. Wipe away any excess oil if necessary. You do not want to wipe all of the oil off. You want a smooth, shiny skillet but you don't want puddles of oil in your pan.

And that is all you need to do. Repeat whenever your skillet looks rusted or dull. General cooking, especially when using oil, will often keep the pan seasoned.

Maintenance

Seasoning your cast iron skillet whenever it looks rusted or dull is the maintenance that you will do on a regular basis. Seasoning the skillet is very important and will help keep your skillet its best.

When it comes to washing your skillet, always rinse the skillet immediately after cooking. Run hot water over it, and wipe it clean. For food that is stuck on, use a non-metal brush and scrub with coarse salt. This will help remove the food without wrecking the skillet.

Dry the skillet thoroughly. Leaving a cast iron skillet wet will cause rust to form on the skillet, and this will shorten the life of your pan. If rust does form, use steel wool to remove the rust. Do not use it on other parts of the skillet. Once the rust is removed, go through the seasoning process with the skillet.

Finally, whenever you wash your skillet, spray it with a small amount cooking oil. Then place a paper towel inside the pan to store.

And that is all you need to do to maintain your cast iron skillet.

Health Benefits

Although you wouldn't think of a skillet as something with health benefits, there are a number of health benefits that you can get by cooking with a cast iron skillet. These health benefits are:

1. You generally use less oil.

Because of how you season a cast iron skillet, you will find that your recipes do not require as much oil as they used to. This means less fat and food that has more flavor than grease. Both will help with your health. For one, you will enjoy the taste of your food and be less inclined to eat out and the other means that your meals are leaner.

2. You are exposed to fewer chemicals.

Cast iron is the natural choice when it comes to cooking. Most skillets that are not cast iron have a spray coating on them to make them non-stick. This coating contains several chemicals including perfluorocarbons, which are released into the air and into your food during cooking.

These chemicals are linked to liver damage, developmental problems in children and cancer.

Cast iron, as long has it has not been coated, is free from those chemicals and does not leave any chemicals in your food.

3. You will have an iron boost.

Finally, cast iron offers an increase of iron in your food, a huge benefit. Many people, especially women, have an iron deficiency. Cooking with cast iron helps boost iron by as much as 20% your daily iron intake.

Cast Iron Cooking Tips

The final thing that I want to touch on before we get into the recipes is to offer a few helpful tips that will make cooking with cast iron much easier. These are:

1. Always Preheat

Make sure that you always preheat your cast iron skillet. It can take a bit of time for the cast iron to heat up, so putting the food in too soon can cause your food to be undercooked or to take longer to cook. Preheating it will ensure that your food is being cooked on the best temperature every time.

2. Cook on Medium Temperatures

Although it does take time for cast iron to heat up, once it does, it maintains its heat for long periods. Cooking on high temperatures will result in your food burning, so always cook on medium temperatures -- medium-low through medium-high.

3. Don't Be Afraid to Make it Versatile

If there is a tool that is truly versatile it's the cast iron skillet. You can use it as a frying pan, a deep fryer, and even as a baking dish. One of the best things is that you can easily move your cast iron skillet from stove top to oven without having to do anything to it.

Experiment with your cast iron, and you will find it is really enjoyable to use. In fact, many of the recipes in this book will have you using your cast iron skillet as more than just a frying pan.

4. Reduce Cooking Times

Whenever you are using a recipe that is not designed for the cast iron skillet, make sure that you reduce cooking times a bit. Remember that the cast iron skillet maintains its heat for quite a while so you can cook the dish almost to completion, turn down the temperature or turn off the stove, and let the pan do the rest of the cooking.

Note: Always watch your food if you are leaving it in the cast iron skillet for serving since the food can burn if the pan is still hot.

5. Watch that Heat

Finally, watch the temperature of the pan. Since the handles are not covered, they will get as hot as the pan itself. It's a good idea to always wear oven mitts when handling your cast iron skillet to prevent burns.

So now that you know the tips; grab your cast iron skillets and let's get started on the recipes!

Recipes

Breakfast Recipes

Star your breakfasts off right with the perfect cast iron skillet breakfast recipes. There is no doubt that these delicious recipes will please even the pickiest person in your house.

Breezy Brunch Skillet

Servings: 6
Preparation time: 10 minutes
Cooking time: 35 minutes

Ingredients:
6 cups of frozen hash browns
6 eggs
6 slices of bacon
1 green pepper
1/2 cup of onion, chopped
1/2 cup of cheddar cheese, shredded
1/4 teaspoon of pepper
1 teaspoon of salt

Preparation:
1. Place a 10" cast iron skillet onto the stove and set the temperature to medium.
2. Chop the bacon, and place it into the skillet.
3. Cook the bacon until it is crispy, usually about 5 to 10 minutes.
4. Drain the bacon, but reserve 2 tablespoons of the bacon grease. You can dispose of the rest.

5. Set aside the bacon, and return the cast iron skillet to the stove without washing it or getting a clean one. You want the flavour of the bacon that will still be in the pan.
6. Add the bacon grease.
7. Wash and seed the green pepper. Chop it.
8. Wash, peel, and chop the onion.
9. Pour the potatoes into the skillet.
10. Add in the green pepper and onion. Stir until the vegetables are well blended.
11. Season with the salt and pepper, and cook for about 2 minutes.
12. Stir the ingredients, and then cover the cast iron skillet with a lid.
13. Cook the vegetables until the hash browns are golden brown, usually about 15 minutes. Make sure that you stir the hash browns every few minutes to prevent burning, but don't over stir them or you will turn the mixture to mush.
14. Once the hash browns are tender, using the back of a wooden spoon, create an indent into the potato. Make 4 indents; one for two eggs.
15. Carefully break an egg into each indentation.
16. Cover the cast iron skillet with the lid again and continue to cook on medium heat until the eggs have the proper consistency, usually about 8 to 10 minutes.
17. Shred the cheese, and toss it with the bacon.
18. When the eggs are cooked to the desired consistency, remove the cast iron skillet from the stove.
19. Sprinkle the dish with cheese and bacon, cover for a minute to allow the cheese to melt slightly, then serve warm.

Steak and Eggs Benedict

Servings: 4
Preparation time: 10 minutes
Cooking time: 20 to 40 minutes

Ingredients:

8 egg yolks
1 tablespoon of black pepper
1 tablespoon of salt
1 16 ounce Strip Steak
3 tablespoons of vegetable oil
8 eggs
1 French Baguette
2 tablespoons of butter
1 cup of butter, unsalted
4 tablespoons of lemon juice
1/4 teaspoon of salt
1/4 teaspoon of white pepper
Dash of Hot Pepper

Preparation:

1. Place a cast iron skillet on the stove, and set to medium high.
2. Add the oil, and heat until sizzling.
3. While the oil is heating, combine the black pepper and tablespoon of salt. Mix thoroughly.
4. Rub the salt mixture onto the steak.
5. Place the steak into the oil, and cook until the steak is medium rare. The best way to do this is to cook the steak for about 3 to 5 minutes on each side. Make sure you only turn the steak once to get the best flavouring.
6. Remove the steak from the heat, and allow to cool slightly before slicing it into 1/2" slices.

7. While the steak is cooling, slice the baguette into 1/2" slices. Toast each piece of baguette. Set to the side.
8. Separate the egg yolks from the egg whites. You can keep the egg whites for a different recipe or throw them away.
9. In a blender, combine the egg yolks and lemon juice.
10. Add the hot sauce, and blend the mixture for about 20 seconds or until it is well blended. Make sure you use the lowest setting as you do not want to make the eggs frothy.
11. Add in the cup of butter, and blend for 2 to 3 minutes or until the butter is fully mixed, and you have a thin mixture.
12. Blend in the white pepper and 1/4 teaspoon of salt. Set aside this mixture as it is a Hollandaise sauce.
13. In a fresh cast iron skillet (the best size is a 10"), add the 2 tablespoons of butter, and place the skillet on the stove set to medium heat.
14. Once the butter is melted, carefully crack the eggs into the pan. Don't overcrowd the eggs. You may have to do the eggs in batches.
15. Cook until the eggs are the desired consistency. With this dish, the yolks should be glossy and the whites should be set.
16. Remove the eggs from the heat.
17. Place a few slices of steak onto each baguette toast.
18. Add a fried egg to the top of the steak. There should only be one egg per baguette toast.
19. Spoon on the Hollandaise sauce, which is the egg yolk and lemon juice mixture that you made in the blender.
20. Serve warm.

Sunny Skillet Breakfast

Servings: 6
Preparation time: 10 minutes
Cooking time: 30 minutes

Ingredients:
3 cups of potatoes
2 tablespoons of vegetable oil
1 onion
1 red bell pepper
6 eggs
1 garlic clove
1 tablespoon of butter
1/4 teaspoon of pepper

Preparation:
1. Preheat the oven to 350°F.
2. Wash and peel the potatoes.
3. Shred the potatoes, and place in a bowl of cold water so the potatoes are completely covered. Let them sit for 5 minutes.
4. While the potatoes are sitting, place a cast iron skillet onto the stove. The best size to use for this meal is a 10" pan.
5. Add the butter, and set the heat to medium.
6. Pour in the oil. Heat the oil and butter.
7. Wash and seed the bell pepper. Dice it into small portions.
8. Wash, peel, and chop the onion.
9. Place both vegetables into the hot pan, and sauté until the onions are tender, usually 3 to 5 minutes.
10. When the onions are cooked, mince the garlic, and add to the onion mixture. Sauté for a minute.

11. Remove the potatoes from the water, and drain them on a paper towel. Place the shredded potatoes into the pan, and mix until the onion mixture is well blended.
12. Continue to grill until the potatoes are golden brown and tender, usually about 10 minutes.
13. Once the potatoes are tender, remove from the heat.
14. Using the back of a wooden spoon, create an indentation in the potato. Make 6 indents; one for each egg.
15. Carefully break an egg into each indentation.
16. Sprinkle the eggs with pepper.
17. Place the cast iron skillet into the oven, and bake the dish for 12 to 14 minutes or until the eggs are the desired consistency.
18. Remove from the oven and serve warm.

Farm House Breakfast

Servings: 4
Preparation time: 20 minutes
Cooking time: 30 minutes

Ingredients:
3 cups of red skinned potatoes
8 eggs
1/4 cup of parsley leaves, chopped and fresh
1/4 teaspoon of black pepper
3 tablespoons of butter
1 teaspoon of salt
2 garlic cloves
1 cup of farmhouse cheddar, shredded

Preparation:
1. Preheat the oven to 400°F.
2. Wash the potatoes, but do not peel them.
3. Chop the potatoes into small hash browns, usually smaller than a half inch.
4. Wash and chop the parsley leaves.
5. Place a 10" to 12" cast iron skillet onto the stove, and set the heat to medium.
6. Add the butter, and allow the butter to melt completely.
7. Place the potatoes into the butter, and sauté for about 15 minutes or until the potatoes are tender and have started to brown.
8. Mince the garlic, and stir into the potatoes, cook for an additional minute.
9. Fold in the salt and pepper.
10. Add the parsley, cook for another minute.
11. Remove the cast iron pan from the stove.
12. Using the back of a wooden spoon, create an indent into the potato. Make 4 indents; one for two eggs.

13. Carefully break two eggs into each indentation.
14. Place in the oven, and bake until the egg whites are cooked. This usually takes about 10 minutes.
15. Once the eggs have the consistency you want, shred the farmhouse cheese.
16. Remove the cast iron skillet from the oven and sprinkle the cheese over the eggs.
17. Return to the oven, and bake for 1 to 2 minutes or until the cheese has melted.
18. Remove from the oven and serve warm.

Spicy Potato Hash Browns

Servings: 4
Preparation time: 25 minutes
Cooking time: 35 minutes

Ingredients:
5 baking potatoes
1/4 teaspoon of black pepper
1/4 teaspoon of onion powder
1/2 teaspoon of salt
1/4 teaspoon of thyme, dried
1 teaspoon of fresh thyme
1/4 cup of vegetable oil
1/4 teaspoon of oregano
1/2 teaspoon of garlic powder
2 teaspoon of minced garlic
1 cup of yellow onion, diced
3 tablespoons of butter
1/4 teaspoon of cayenne pepper

Preparation:
1. Wash the potatoes, and place them in a pot.
2. Fill with water, and place on the stove set to high.
3. Bring to a boil, and cook the potatoes until they are half cooked, usually about 15 minutes after the water boils.
4. Drain the water, and allow the potatoes to cool.
5. Remove the skins from the potatoes while they are still warm.
6. Chop the potatoes into 1/2" hash browns.
7. Wash, peel, and dice the yellow onions.
8. Mince the fresh garlic
9. Place the 12" cast iron skillet onto the stove and set the temperature to high.
10. Pour in the oil.

11. Add the butter, and heat thoroughly. Add the onions.
12. Sauté the onions until they begin to tender, usually about 3 to 5 minutes.
13. Add the minced garlic to the onions, stirring for about a minute or until the smell of garlic grows strong.
14. Fold in the potatoes, and stir until the potatoes are mixed well with the onions.
15. Chop the fresh thyme, and add it to the potatoes along with the salt and pepper.
16. Sprinkle on the dried thyme, oregano, onion powder, garlic powder and cayenne pepper. Do not stir in the ingredients. Simply shake the pan to keep the potatoes from burning.
17. Allow the ingredients to cook until the bottom of the potatoes are golden brown, usually about 4 to 6 minutes.
18. Using a spatula, turn the potatoes.
19. Cook on the other side until the potatoes are golden brown throughout, usually an additional 4 minutes.
20. Remove from heat and serve warm.

Caprese Skillet Eggs

Servings: 4
Preparation time: 10 minutes
Cooking time: 20 minutes

Ingredients:

3 tomatoes
1/2 cup of onion, copped
4 eggs
2 tablespoons of olive oil
1/2 teaspoon of salt
4 teaspoons of fresh oregano
4 teaspoons of fresh chives
4 teaspoons of fresh basil
1/2 teaspoon of pepper
1/2 cup of mozzarella cheese

Preparation:

1. Wash the tomatoes, and chop into bite-sized pieces.
2. Wash, peel, and chop the onion.
3. Place a 10" cast iron skillet onto the stove, and set to medium heat.
4. Pour in the oil and heat.
5. Once the oil is hot, place in the chopped onion.
6. Sauté the onion until it is tender and almost translucent; between 3 to 5 minutes.
7. Fold in the tomatoes and season with the salt and pepper.
8. Cook the vegetables for about 5 minutes, or until the tomatoes are soft. Stir frequently while cooking.
9. Once the tomatoes are soft, using a wooden spoon, make an indentation in the tomato mixture.
10. Repeat until you have four wells or indentations in the tomatoes.
11. Carefully crack an egg into each well.

12. Place a lid on the cast iron skillet, and continue to cook until the whites are firm and the yolks are still soft. This can take anywhere from 5 to 10 minutes.
13. Shred the mozzarella cheese
14. Once the eggs are the desired consistency, sprinkle the dish with the shredded cheese.
15. Return the lid to the skillet, and cook for an additional minute.
16. Wash and chop the oregano, basil, and chives. Toss together.
17. Remove from heat, and sprinkle the herbs on top.
18. Serve on its own or with toast.

Berry Pancakes

Servings: 4
Preparation time: 10 minutes
Cooking time: 20 minutes

Ingredients:
1 cup of flour, all purpose
1/4 cup of white sugar
1 cup of milk
2 tablespoons of butter, unsalted
4 eggs
1/4 teaspoon of salt
1/2 teaspoon of lemon zest
1/2 cup of blueberries
1/2 cup of raspberries

Preparation:
1. Preheat the oven to 400°F.
2. Sift the flour into a bowl.
3. Zest the lemon, and add to the flour.
4. Add the salt.
5. In a separate bowl, whisk together the eggs and milk.
6. Slowly add the egg mixture to the flour mixture. Mix until the ingredients are well blended and you have a smooth batter.
7. Wash and stem the blueberries. Place in a separate bowl.
8. Wash and cut the raspberries in half. Place the raspberries in the same bowl as the blueberries, and toss the fruit together.
9. Place a cast iron skillet onto the stove, and set the heat to high. Make sure that you use a 12" skillet.
10. When the skillet is hot, add the butter and allow it to melt.

11. Once the butter is melted, pour the batter into the hot skillet. Turn the skillet slightly to make sure the batter covers the entire pan.
12. Add the berry mixture to the top of the batter. You should scatter the berries so they are all over the entire batter. Don't worry if the berries sink into the batter.
13. Remove from the stove, and place the cast iron skillet into the oven.
14. Bake for 20 minutes or until the pastry is baked completely through and is puffed.
15. Remove from the oven, serve warm with syrup, icing sugar, or whipped cream.

Breakfast Scramble

Servings: 6
Preparation time: 5 minutes
Cooking time: 10 minutes

Ingredients:
12 eggs
1 red onion
1 jalapeno
2 tablespoons of chives, diced
2 tablespoons of butter, unsalted
1/4 teaspoon of salt
1/4 teaspoon of black pepper
1/2 cup of goat cheese (1/2 cup of feta cheese or cheddar cheese as a substitute for goat cheese)

Preparation:
1. Place a large, 12" cast iron skillet on the stove, and set the heat to medium.
2. Wash, peel, and dice the red onion.
3. Wash and cut the jalapeno into circles. Keep the seeds with the cut pepper.
4. Add the butter to the skillet and melt.
5. Pour in the onion and jalapeno, and sauté for about 5 to 7 minutes or until the peppers and onions are soft.
6. In a separate bowl, whisk together the eggs.
7. Whisk in the salt and pepper.
8. Pour the eggs into the skillet and cook, stirring frequently, until you have the desired consistency. Usually takes about 3 to 5 minutes.
9. While the eggs are cooking, crumble the goat cheese. If you are using cheddar cheese, shred it, or crumble the feta cheese.
10. Wash and dice the fresh chives.
11. Remove the eggs from the stove and fold in the cheese and chives.
12. Serve warm.

Main Dishes/Entree Recipes

Often, we get stuck in a rut when it comes to weekly menus. It can be difficult to come up with main dishes that offer the variety we wish for. However, once you have a cast iron skillet, you will find that there is a whole range of variety and you can really explore new tastes with your main dishes.

Poultry

Chicken and Dressings

Servings: 6
Preparation time: 15 minutes
Cooking time: 50 minutes

Ingredients:
3 cups of chicken, cubed
1 teaspoon of salt
1 teaspoon of pepper
1 cup of celery
2 eggs
1 cup of frozen corn
1 cup of onion, chopped
2 tablespoons of butter
1 /12 teaspoon of poultry seasoning
2 packages of Buttermilk Cornbread Mix (6ounce packages)
2 tablespoons of vegetable oil
1 3/4 cups of milk

Preparation:

1. Preheat the oven to 400°F.
2. Wash, peel, and chop onion.
3. Wash and chop celery.
4. In a bowl, toss together the salt, pepper and raw chicken.
5. Add 1 tablespoon of oil to a cast iron skillet, and place on a stove. Set temperature to medium.
6. Cube the chicken, and add it to the skillet. Fry until the chicken is fully cooked, about 10 to 15 minutes.
7. Remove chicken from heat, and set aside to cool.
8. Add the butter to a 10" cast iron skillet. You can use the one you cooked the chicken in or a clean skillet.
9. Melt the butter on medium heat.
10. Toss the onion and celery together, and add to the cast iron skillet.
11. Cook for about 10 minutes or until the celery and onions are tender.
12. Remove from heat, and pour the celery mixture into a bowl. Set aside.
13. Pour the oil into the cast iron skillet, and place in the oven.
14. Heat for 5 minutes.
15. While the cast iron skillet is heating, mix together the cornbread and chicken.
16. Fold in the poultry seasoning.
17. Toss in the onions and celery.
18. Add the corn and toss until all the ingredients are well blended.
19. In a separate bowl, whisk together the milk and eggs.
20. Add it to the vegetable mixture, and mix well.
21. Remove the cast iron skillet from the oven.
22. Pour the vegetable batter into the skillet.
23. Place back in the oven, and bake for 30 to 35 minutes. You will want the dish to be golden brown.
24. Serve warm.

Spinach Stuffed Sundried Tomato Chicken

Serves: 4
Preparation time: 15 minutes
Cooking time: 40 minutes

Ingredients:

4 boneless, skinless chicken breasts, split along the side
½ cup bacon, diced
2 cloves garlic, crushed and minced
2 cups spinach, chopped
½ cup jarred sundried tomatoes, chopped
1 cup seasoned bread crumbs
½ cup parmesan cheese, freshly grated
¼ cup fresh parsley, chopped
2 eggs, beaten
1 teaspoon salt
1 teaspoon black pepper
1 cup red onion, chopped
4 cups sweet potato, cubed
¼ teaspoon nutmeg
¼ teaspoon oregano
½ teaspoon paprika
1 tablespoon olive oil
1 cup chicken stock
1 cup smoked provolone cheese, shredded

Preparation:

1. Preheat oven to 375°F.
2. Prepare a 12-inch cast iron skillet and add the bacon over medium heat. Cook until bacon is semi crisp, approximately 5 minutes.
3. Add the garlic and sauté for 1 minute before adding the spinach and sundried tomatoes. Sauté, stirring gently for 2-3 minutes. Using a slotted spoon, transfer the mixture to a bowl and set aside to cool slightly.
4. Add the sweet potatoes and onion to the skillet and cook, stirring occasionally, for 5 minutes. Season with nutmeg, oregano, and paprika. Cook an additional 3 minutes before removing from the pan. Add the olive oil to the pan and keep the heat on medium.
5. In a bowl, combine the seasoned bread crumbs, parmesan cheese, fresh parsley, salt and black pepper.
6. Stuff each chicken breast with equal amounts of the spinach mixture. Baste each piece of chicken with the beaten egg, and then dredge through the bread crumb mixture.
7. Place the chicken in the pan and cook until lightly browned on each side, approximately 3-4 minutes.
8. Add the sweet potatoes back into the pan and add the chicken stock. Cover the chicken with shredded provolone cheese.
9. Place the skillet in the oven and bake for 20-25 minutes, or until chicken is cooked through and juices run clear.

Roasted Rosemary Chicken

Servings: 6
Preparation time: 15 minutes
Cooking time: 1 hour 30 minutes

Ingredients:
1 large roasting chicken (4-5 pounds)
6 fresh rosemary springs
1 teaspoon of paprika
1 tablespoons of kosher salt
¼ cup of olive oil
1 teaspoon dry thyme
2 tablespoons of lemon juice
2 tablespoons of butter
1/4 teaspoon of sea salt
2 teaspoons of minced garlic
24 pearl onions, trimmed
1 cup dry white wine
12 white mushrooms, trimmed and quartered

Preparation:
1. Pre-heat the oven to 450°F
2. Rinse your chicken inside out with cold running water. Use paper towels to pat dry the chicken inside and out. Chicken must be dry if you want a crispy skinned chicken.
3. Season the cavity of the chicken with the kosher salt and place two of the rosemary springs inside.
4. Chop rosemary of two springs.
5. Mix the chopped rosemary, garlic, olive oil, pepper, paprika, lemon juice and thyme in a small mixing bowl. Stir until well combined.
6. Place your largest cast iron skillet on the stove, and set to medium high.

7. Add the butter. Add the pearl onions when the butter is melted. Sauté the onions until they are fragrant and almost tender, about 3-4 minutes. Remove from heat.

8. Place the chicken, breasts side up, in the cast iron skillet, pushing the onions on the side. Add the mushrooms. Brush generously the chicken, and mushrooms with the rosemary and olive oil mixture. Place two rosemary springs on the chicken. Tie the chicken legs with kitchen twine.

9. Place the skillet in the pre-heated oven. Let the chicken roast for 1h15, until the chicken is well cooked and the juices run clear when you slit the thigh skin. To make certain your chicken is well cook, insert a meat thermometer in the breast without touching any bones. The internal temperature should read 165°F.

10. Remove the chicken from the oven and place the chicken on a serving plate with the onions and mushrooms while you prepare the sauce. Cover the chicken loosely with aluminum foil to keep it warm.

11. Place the cast iron skillet on the stove on high heat, and quickly add the white wine. Bring to a boil. Let the sauce reduce by half. It should take about 5 minutes. Make sure to scrap all the bits of flavour from the chicken and the onions from the bottom of the skillet with a spoon as the sauce is reducing. Keep the sauce warm until ready to serve.

12. When ready to serve, carve your chicken and place the sauce in a saucer. Serve warm with pearl onions and mushrooms.

Chicken Pot Pie

Servings: 6
Preparation time: 10 minutes
Cooking time: 35 minutes

Ingredients:
4 cups of chicken, cooked and shredded (about 5 to 6 chicken breasts)
1/3 cup of butter
1 tablespoon of oil
2 tablespoons of butter
1 cup of carrots, diced
1 cup of mushrooms, sliced
1/3 cup of flour, all purpose
1 1/2 cups of chicken broth
1 cup of frozen sweet peas
2 cups of frozen hash browns
1 1/2 cups of milk
1 1/2 teaspoons of Creole seasoning
1 onion
1/3 cup of fresh parsley
1 egg white
2 premade piecrusts

Preparation:
1. Add 1 tablespoon of oil to a cast iron skillet, and place on a stove. Set temperature to medium.
2. Cut the chicken into smaller strips to help with cooking, and add it to the skillet. Fry until the chicken is fully cooked, about 10 to 15 minutes.
3. Remove from heat and cool.
4. Once cool, place in a blender, and shred the chicken. Set aside.
5. Preheat the oven to 350°F.

6. Place a large saucepan onto the stove, and set to medium heat.
7. Add the 1/3 cup of butter and melt.
8. Once the butter is melted, stir in the flour. Cook for about 1 minute, stirring continuously.
9. Stir in the chicken broth.
10. Add in the milk. Continue to cook until the ingredients become thick; usually about 6 to 7 minutes.
11. Remove from heat, and stir in the Creole seasoning. Set aside.
12. In a separate cast iron skillet, melt 2 tablespoons of butter on a medium-high heat.
13. Wash, peel, and chop the onions. Place in the skillet.
14. Wash and chop the mushrooms, add to the onions.
15. Sauté the mushrooms and onions for about 10 minutes, or until they are tender.
16. Fold in the shredded chicken.
17. Wash, peel, and chop the carrots into matchsticks. Add to the onion mixture.
18. Stir in the peas, and frozen hash browns.
19. Chop the parsley, and mix into the skillet.
20. Cook for about 2 to 4 minutes until the ingredients are heated.
21. Pour in the sauce and mix well.
22. Remove from heat.
23. In a clean and lightly greased, 10" cast iron skillet, place one of the piecrusts into the bottom of the skillet. Remember to remove the pie plate if it is sold with one.
24. Pour the chicken mixture into the piecrust until it is filled.
25. Top with the remaining piecrust, again, making sure you remove the pie plate if it has one.
26. Separate the egg white from the egg yolk. Throw away the egg yolk, or use it for a different recipe.
27. Brush the egg white over the top pie crust.
28. Cut 5 slits into the top of the pie.
29. Place in the oven for 1 hour or until the pie crust is golden brown and the mixture is bubbling.
30. Serve warm.

Dijon and Wine Roasted Chicken

Serves: 4-6
Preparation time: 15 minutes
Cooking time: 1 hour

Ingredients:

2 pounds assorted chicken pieces, bone-in, with skin
½ cup pancetta, cubed
¼ cup shallots, sliced
2 cup Brussels sprouts, halved
¼ cup Dijon mustard
1 tablespoon Herbs de Provence
1 teaspoon salt
1 teaspoon ground peppercorns
½ cup flour
1 cup chicken stock
½ cup dry white wine

Preparation:

1. Preheat the oven to 350°F.
2. Prepare a 12-inch cast iron skillet and add the pancetta over medium heat. Cook the pancetta until crispy, approximately 5 minutes.
3. Add the shallots and cook while stirring for 1-2 minutes more before adding the Brussels sprouts and cooking, stirring frequently, for an additional five minutes.
4. Using a slotted spoon, remove the Brussels sprouts, shallots and pancetta. Set aside.
5. In a bowl, combine the Herbs de Provence, salt, and ground peppercorns with the flour. Mix well.
6. Brush the chicken with the Dijon mustard and then dredge lightly in the flour mixture.

7. Place the chicken back in the skillet and using the residual grease from the pancetta (add additional olive oil, if needed) brown the chicken on both sides over medium heat.
8. Add the white wine and reduce for 2 minutes, then add the chicken stock to the skillet followed by the Brussels sprouts and pancetta.
9. Place the skillet in the oven and bake for 35-40 minutes, or until chicken is crispy brown and cooked through to at least 165°F internal temperature.
10. Transfer to serving plates and drizzle with pan sauce before serving.

Sage Roasted Chicken with Rustic Vegetables

Serves: 4
Preparation time: 10 minutes
Cooking time: 50 minutes

Ingredients:
4 bone-in chicken breasts
½ cup olive oil
2 cups red potatoes, halved
2 cups whole mini portabella mushrooms
1 cup red onion, cut into thick slices
4 cloves garlic, crushed and minced
½ cup chicken stock
1 tablespoon lemon juice
1 tablespoon whole sage leaves
1 teaspoon salt
1 teaspoon ground black peppercorns
1 lemon sliced

Preparation:
1. Preheat oven to 400°F.
2. Prepare a 12-inch cast iron skillet and heat olive oil over medium.
3. Add the chicken and cook on one side for 3 minutes. Turn the chicken and add the red potatoes, portabella mushrooms, red onion, and garlic. Continue cooking for 5-7 minutes, or until chicken is browned on the outside.
4. Add the chicken stock, lemon juice, whole sage, salt, and ground peppercorns. Toss lightly to mix. Place the lemon slices over the chicken and vegetables.
5. Place in the oven and bake for 40 minutes, or until chicken is cooked through and juices run clear.

Spicy Chicken and Lemongrass Peanut Noodles

Serves: 4
Preparation time: 10 minutes
Cooking time: 20 minutes

Ingredients:
1 pound boneless skinless chicken breast, cubed
2 teaspoons olive oil
½ cup soy sauce
3 cloves garlic, crushed and minced
1 tablespoon fresh ginger, grated
1 tablespoon fresh lemongrass, chopped
1 tablespoon chili garlic paste
½ cup creamy natural peanut butter
1 tablespoon lime juice
2 teaspoons sesame oil
2 cups chicken stock
½ pound angel hair pasta
½ cup peanuts, chopped
Scallions, sliced for garnish

Preparation:
1. Prepare a 12-inch cast iron skillet and add the olive oil over medium heat.
2. Add the chicken and sauté until browned, approximately 5 minutes.
3. Add the soy sauce, garlic, ginger, lemon grass, and chili garlic paste. Stir in with the chicken and cook 1-2 minutes.
4. Add the peanut butter, lime juice, sesame oil, and chicken stock. Turn heat up to medium high until the stock boils. Add the angel hair pasta and reduce the heat to simmer. Cook 5-7 minutes, or until noodles are tender.
5. Remove from heat and add peanuts before serving.

Basil Balsamic Baked Chicken

Serves: 4
Preparation time: 5 minutes
Cooking time: 30 minutes

Ingredients:

1 ½ pounds boneless, skinless chicken breast
1 tablespoon olive oil
1 cup red onion, sliced
2 cups small red potatoes, halved
2 cups sugar snap peas, washed and trimmed
3 cloves garlic, crushed and minced
1 cup chicken stock
¼ cup balsamic vinegar
¼ cup heavy cream
1 tablespoon honey
1 sprig fresh rosemary
¼ cup fresh basil, chopped
1 teaspoon salt
1 teaspoon black pepper

Preparation:

1. Preheat oven to 400°F.
2. Prepare a 12-inch cast iron skillet and heat the olive oil over medium heat.
3. Add the chicken and brown on both sides, approximately 3-5 minutes per side. Remove from pan and set aside.
4. Add the red potatoes, sugar snap peas, and garlic. Sauté just until potatoes begin to brown, approximately 5 minutes. Add more olive oil, if needed. Remove from the pan and keep with the chicken.
5. Add the balsamic vinegar to the pan and reduce, scraping the skillet while you do so, for 1-2 minutes.

6. Stir in the chicken stock, heavy cream and honey, stirring constantly. Season with rosemary, basil, salt, and black pepper.
7. Add the chicken back into the skillet, followed by the vegetables.
8. Place the skillet in the oven and bake 20 minutes or until chicken is cooked through and juices run clear.

Old World Chicken Parmesan

Serves: 4
Preparation time: 10 minutes
Cooking time: 30 minutes

Ingredients:
4 boneless, skinless chicken breasts, pounded thin
¼ cup olive oil
3 cloves garlic, crushed and minced
¼ cup shallots, sliced
2 teaspoons fresh rosemary, chopped
¼ cup fresh basil, chopped
2 teaspoons fresh thyme, chopped
¼ cup fresh parsley, chopped
1 teaspoon salt
1 teaspoon black pepper
¼ cup dry red wine
2 ½ cups tomato or marinara sauce
½ pound dry vermicelli noodles
1 cup fresh mozzarella cheese, shredded
½ cup parmesan cheese, freshly grated

Preparation:
1. Preheat oven to 450°F.
2. Prepare a 12-inch cast iron skillet and heat the olive oil over medium heat.
3. Add the chicken and cook on both sides, until lightly browned, approximately 2-3 minutes per side.
4. Add the garlic and shallots. Season the chicken with the rosemary, basil, thyme, parsley, salt, and black pepper. Add the red wine and let reduce for 1-2 minutes.

5. Add tomato or marinara sauce, stirring gently and spooning over the chicken. Break the vermicelli noodles in half and spread them around in the sauce. Simmer for 3 minutes and remove from heat.
6. Top the chicken first with the mozzarella cheese and then the parmesan cheese.
7. Place in the oven and bake for 20 minutes, or until cheese is bubbly and slightly golden.
8. Let cool slightly before serving.

Kung Pao Chicken

Serves: 4
Preparation time: 10 minutes
Cooking time: 20 minutes

Ingredients

4 x 4 ounce chicken breast, skinless, boneless
1 teaspoon fresh ginger, grated
½ cup shallots, diced
½ cup low-sodium soy sauce
2 teaspoons brown sugar
½ teaspoon cornstarch
1 green chili pepper, seeded, minced
Extra virgin olive oil

Preparation:

1. Cube chicken into ¾" pieces.
2. Heat 4 tablespoons oil in cast iron deep skillet over medium heat, add chicken breast, and brown. Remove from skillet, and set aside.
3. Into same skillet, add shallots, ginger, pepper, sauté for 2 minutes, ensure ginger does not brown too quickly.
4. Stir in cornstarch, brown sugar, pour in a little soy sauce to deglaze skillet, return chicken to skillet, mix in corn starch.
5. Reduce heat and simmer on low for 10 minutes.
6. Serve Kung Pao Chicken with white rice.

Crispy Coconut Chicken Tenders

Serve: 4
Preparation time: 15 minutes
Cooking time: 10 minutes

Ingredients:

4 x 4 ounce chicken breast, skinless, boneless
1½ cups flour
½ cup shredded coconut
2 tablespoons milk
2 eggs
1 teaspoon oregano
1 teaspoon paprika
1 teaspoon thyme
1 teaspoon salt and black pepper
Extra virgin olive oil

Preparation:

1. Whisk eggs in bowl, add milk, mix.
2. In a second shallow bowl, combine flour with spices.
3. In a third shallow bowl, place shredded coconut.
4. Slice chicken breast into 2"-wide chicken strips.
5. Dip each strip in egg mixture, then coat in flour mixture, next drip in coconut mixture.
6. Heat 4 tablespoons oil in cast iron deep skillet over medium heat, drop chicken strips into skillet, and cook for 3-4 minutes per side or until no longer pink inside.
7. Serve with lemon garlic dipping sauce (recipe follow).

Lemon Garlic Dipping Sauce

Serve: 6
Preparation time: 5 minutes
Cooking time: 2 minutes

Ingredients:

1 cup mayonnaise

1/3 cup lemon juice

2 cloves garlic, grated

1 teaspoon coarse black pepper

1 teaspoon salt

Preparation:

1. Place ingredients in blender, and mix until smooth.
2. Refrigerate for 30 minutes before serving.

Honey Garlic Chicken Thighs with Broccoli Slaw

Serves: 4
Preparation time: 15 minutes
Cooking time: 30 minutes

Ingredients:
8 chicken thighs, skinless, boneless
½ cup honey
6 cloves garlic, minced
1 cup low-sodium chicken stock
¼ cup soy sauce
Extra virgin olive oil

Broccoli Slaw
1 head broccoli
½ cup carrots, grated
¼ cup raisins
¼ cup peanuts or cashews
½ cup low-fat mayonnaise
1 teaspoon black pepper
½ teaspoon salt

Preparation:
1. Heat 3 tablespoons olive oil in a large cast iron skillet over medium heat. Add chicken thighs, and brown.
2. Add garlic, honey, and soy sauce, stir to coat thighs. Cook thighs about a minute per side in honey sauce.
3. Add chicken stock, bring to simmer, reduce heat to medium-low, cover with a lid or foil and cook for 25 minutes or until chicken is no longer pink inside.
4. For slaw, peel broccoli stalk and grate broccoli using food processor.
5. Combine grated broccoli with remaining ingredients and refrigerate for 20 minutes before serving.
6. Serve Honey Garlic Chicken Thighs with Broccoli Slaw

Orange Ginger Chicken

Servings: 4
Preparation time: 15 minutes
Cooking time: 20 minutes

Ingredients:

1 pound of chicken breast, boneless, skinless (usually 3 breasts)
2 oranges
2 tablespoons of soy sauce, separated
2 garlic cloves
1/2 cup of cornstarch plus 2 teaspoons
2 teaspoons of dry sherry
1/4 teaspoon of crushed red pepper
2 cups of canola oil plus 1 tablespoon
2 tablespoons of sugar
1 teaspoon of rice vinegar
2 teaspoon of fresh garlic, minced

Preparation:

1. Slice the chicken into 1 1/2" slices. Place in a bowl.
2. Add one tablespoon of soy sauce and 1 teaspoon of sherry. Toss until the chicken is coated.
3. Place in the fridge, and allow it to stand for about 30 minutes.
4. Place a 10" cast iron skillet onto the stove, and set temperature to medium.
5. Pour in enough of the 2 cups of oil to fill the pan about a 1/2". You may not need the full 2 cups.
6. Add 1/2 cup of cornstarch to a small bowl.
7. Remove the chicken from the sauce, and dip it in the cornstarch. Turn the chicken until it is completely coated. Knock off any excess cornstarch.
8. Place the chicken into the hot oil. Do not overcrowd. You may have to do several batches.

9. Cook the chicken, turning several times, until it is a deep golden brown and is cooked completely through. This usually takes about 5 to 10 minutes.
10. Remove chicken from the oil and drain on paper towel.
11. Use a vegetable peeler, and make 4 strips of orange zests. You want them to be about 3" to 4" in length.
12. Place the zest between two layers of paper towels.
13. Microwave the zests for about 80 seconds. Make sure you microwave for 20 second intervals, checking the zest after each interval. You want the zest to be dry but not brown.
14. Remove from microwave and cool completely.
15. Once the zest is cooled, dice it, and set it aside.
16. Squeeze the juice from both oranges. Use additional oranges if necessary. You'll need about a 1/2 cup of juice.
17. Pour the juice into a bowl, and add 2 teaspoons of cornstarch. Stir until the cornstarch is completely dissolved. Set aside.
18. In a separate 10" cast iron skillet, heat 1 tablespoon of oil. Set the temperature to medium heat.
19. Mince the garlic, and add it to the skillet.
20. Peel and mince the ginger, and add to the skillet.
21. Stir in the dried orange zest and the crushed red pepper.
22. Sauté for about 30 seconds or until the spices are golden brown.
23. Whisk together the soy sauce and sugar.
24. Add the vinegar and sherry and mix thoroughly.
25. Pour into the garlic mixture, and stir until the sugar has completely dissolved.
26. Add the orange juice mixture.
27. Bring the garlic mixture to a boil, and then reduce heat to low. Simmer for a minute, stirring continuously.
28. Slowly add the fried chicken, adding water if it is too thick. Stir constantly until the dish is hot, and the chicken is coated. This usually takes about 3 to 5 minutes.
29. Serve warm with a favorite side such as rice.

Sausage-and-Chicken Cassoulet

Servings: 4
Preparation time: 20 minutes
Cooking time: 55 minutes

Ingredients:
1 pound of chicken breasts, boneless, skinless (about 3 breasts)
1 pound of smoked sausages (about 6 to 8 sausages)
1 package of buttermilk cornbread mix (1 - 6ounce package)
2 cups of Northern beans (1 - 15.8ounce can)
1 3/4 cups of diced tomatoes with onion and garlic (1 -14.5ounce can)
1 1/2 teaspoons of dried thyme
2/3 cup of milk
1 3/4 cups of chicken broth (1 -14ounce can)

Preparation:
1. Preheat the oven to 400°F.
2. Slice the sausages.
3. Cube the chicken.
4. Place a 12" cast iron skillet onto the stove. Set the temperature to medium.
5. Add the sausages to the pan and cook until they are browned. Usually takes about 8 to 10 minutes.
6. Remove from the heat, and drain the sausages on paper towels. Leave the drippings in the skillet.
7. Return the skillet to the stove, and add the chicken. Cook until the chicken is brown and there is no pink in the middle. This usually takes about 5 to 10 minutes.
8. When the chicken is cooked, add the sausage.
9. Drain and rinse the beans, add to the chicken mixture.
10. Stir in the chicken broth.
11. Add the thyme.

12. Drain the tomatoes, and then add them to the chicken mixture.
13. Bring all the ingredients to a boil, stirring occasionally.
14. Remove from heat.
15. In a separate bowl, toss together the cornbread mix and the milk. Mix until you have a nice smooth batter.
16. Pour the batter over the hot chicken mixture. Make sure it is poured evenly.
17. Place the cast iron skillet into the oven and bake for 30 to 35 minutes or until the cornbread is golden brown.
18. Remove from the oven and let stand for 10 minutes.
19. Serve warm.

Baked Asiago Chicken and Mushroom Pasta

Serves: 4
Preparation time: 10 minutes
Cooking time: 35 minutes

Ingredients:

4 chicken breast, skinless, boneless
½ cup Asiago cheese
8 Crimini mushrooms, stemmed
1 cup low-sodium chicken stock
¼ cup butter
2 teaspoons salt
1½ cup penne

Preparation:

1. Bring pot of salted water to boil, and cook pasta al dente.
2. Preheat oven to 350°F, quarter mushrooms, set aside.
3. Sprinkle chicken breasts with salt and slice against the grain into ½" wide strips.
4. Melt butter in a cast iron deep skillet, add chicken breast, brown.
5. Add mushroom, sauté for 2 minutes.
6. Add chicken stock, pasta, and sprinkle with Asiago cheese.
7. Cover skillet with aluminum foil, and bake in oven for 20 minutes.
8. Serve chicken with pasta.

Buffalo Chicken and Ranch Rice

Serves: 4
Preparation time: 10 minutes
Cooking time: 30 minutes

Ingredients:

4 boneless, skinless chicken breasts
½ cup bacon, diced
1 cup red onion, diced
1 cup celery, diced
1 cup carrots, diced
4 cups cooked rice
2 cups chicken stock
2 teaspoons fresh dill
¼ cup fresh parsley, chopped
1 teaspoon onion powder
1 teaspoon salt
1 teaspoon black pepper
¼-½ cup buffalo sauce, depending on taste preference
½ cup blue cheese crumbles

Preparation:

1. Preheat oven to 400°F.
2. Prepare a 12-inch cast iron skillet and add the bacon over medium heat. Cook until browned, approximately 5 minutes.
3. Add the red onion, celery, and carrots. Sauté for 5 minutes before removing with a slotted spoon. Set aside.
4. Add the chicken to the skillet and brown on each side for 3-5 minutes. Add the sautéed vegetables back into the skillet, along with the rice and chicken stock. Mix well.
5. Season with dill, parsley, onion powder, salt, and black pepper. Add the buffalo sauce and blue cheese. Mix gently.
6. Place in the oven and bake for 20 minutes or until chicken is cooked through and juices run clear.

Cornish Game Hen with Bacon and Onions

Servings: 4
Preparation time: 15 minutes
Cooking time: 30 minutes

Ingredients:

2 Cornish Game Hens (you want ones that are about 1 1/4 pounds)
4 pieces of thick sliced bacon
24 pearl onions
1 teaspoon of salt
1 teaspoon of black pepper

Preparation:

1. Preheat the oven to 500°F.
2. Wrap a brick in aluminum foil so it is completely covered.
3. Place in the oven to heat thoroughly.
4. While the brick is heating, cut the game hen from the tailbone to the neck. Remove the backbone of the hen.
5. Next, fold the game hen open like a book and remove the keel bone.
6. Slice small slits into the skin just above the legs and tuck the drumsticks into the slits. This will keep your game hen from falling apart.
7. Repeat with the second game hen.
8. Season the game hens thoroughly with salt and pepper. Use as much or as little salt and pepper as you like. The recipe calls for 1 teaspoon of each, but you can use more if you like a saltier meat and less if you prefer the opposite.
9. Place a 12" cast iron skillet onto the stove, and set the temperature to medium.
10. Fry the bacon until it is crisp, usually about 5 minutes.

11. Reserve 1 tablespoon of fat from the bacon and remove the bacon. Set the bacon and reserved fat to the side, and drain the skillet.
12. Crumble the bacon.
13. Return the skillet to the stove.
14. Wash and peel the pearl onions. Place the whole onion into the skillet along with the tablespoon of drippings from the bacon.
15. Add the game hens to the pan, skin side up. You want the onions to be around the edges and not under the hen as you want the hens to be directly against the skillet.
16. Remove the brick from the oven, carefully, and place on top of the game hens. You may need to use 2 bricks depending on the size of your bricks.
17. Continue to cook on the stove for about 5 minutes.
18. Place the skillet, bricks and all, into the oven, and bake for 10 to 15 minutes. Use a meat thermometer and check the thigh meat. Once it reaches 170°F, the game hen is finished.
19. Remove from oven, and allow the bricks to cool slightly before removing them, about 5 minutes.
20. Serve the game hen warm, sprinkled with bacon and garnished with the cooked pearl onions.

Ranch Chicken Mac and Cheese

Servings: 6
Preparation time: 15 minutes
Cooking time: 55 minutes

Ingredients:

3 cups of chicken, cooked
1 onion
1 green pepper
2 tablespoons of butter
1/2 cup of sour cream
1 cup of cream cheese (1-8ounce package)
1 cup of cellentani pasta
1 teaspoon of chili powder
1/2 teaspoon of cumin, ground
1 1/4 cup of diced tomatoes with green chilies (1 -10ounce can)
1 1/4 cup of cream of chicken soup (1 - 10ounce can)
1 1/2 cups of cheddar cheese, shredded
1 tablespoons of oil

Preparation:

1. Preheat the oven to 350°F.
2. Add 1 tablespoon of oil to a cast iron skillet and place on a stove. Set temperature to medium.
3. Cut the chicken into smaller strips, and add it to the skillet. Fry until the chicken is fully cooked, about 10 to 15 minutes.
4. Remove from heat and cool.
5. Fill a large pot with water, and set on the stove with the temperature at high.
6. Bring the water to a boil, and add the cellentani pasta. Cook until the pasta is tender.
7. Remove from heat and drain.

8. While the pasta is cooking, place a 12" cast iron skillet onto the stove. Set temperature to medium.
9. Melt the butter in the skillet.
10. Wash, peel, and chop the onion.
11. Wash, seed, and chop the green pepper. Add both vegetables to the hot butter.
12. Sauté until the vegetables are tender, usually between 5 to 10 minutes
13. Fold in the canned tomatoes with green chilies.
14. Cut up the cream cheese and add to the vegetables.
15. Stir for about 2 minutes.
16. Add the chicken, and stir until it is fully incorporated.
17. Fold in the cumin and chili powder.
18. Stir constantly as you work over the hot stove to prevent the mixture from burning.
19. Stir in the sour cream and the cream of chicken soup.
20. Finally, add the cooked pasta, and stir until the ingredients are fully incorporated.
21. Remove from the heat.
22. Shred the cheddar cheese, and sprinkle the top of the pasta.
23. Place in the oven, and bake for 25 to 30 minutes.
24. Remove from the oven and serve warm.

Creamy Chicken Enchilada Skillet

Serves: 4-6
Preparation time: 10 minutes
Cooking time: 20 minutes

Ingredients:

1 pound boneless, skinless chicken breast, cubed
1 tablespoon olive oil
3 cloves garlic, crushed and minced
1 teaspoon chili powder
½ teaspoon cumin
1 teaspoon salt
1 teaspoon black pepper
1 cup white mushrooms, sliced
2 cups spinach, torn
1 cup black beans (canned or precooked)
1 ½ cups cooked rice
2 cups salsa verde or green enchilada sauce, divided
½ cup sour cream
¼ cup cream cheese, softened
6-8 flour or corn tortillas
½ cup Monterey Jack cheese
½ cup Mexican queso cheese
Fresh cilantro for garnish

Preparation:

1. Preheat the broiler.
2. Prepare a 12-inch cast iron skillet and heat the olive oil over medium heat.
3. Add the chicken and cook, while stirring, until chicken is browned, approximately 5 minutes.
4. Add the garlic and season with chili powder, cumin, salt, and black pepper. Stir to mix.

5. Add the mushrooms and spinach, sauté for 2-3 minutes before adding the black beans and rice. Stir well.
6. In a bowl combine 1 cup of the salsa verde, sour cream and cream cheese. Mix until creamy, add to the skillet and stir.
7. Cover the contents of the skillet with the flour or corn tortillas, in one or two layers over each other.
8. Add the remaining salsa verde on top, followed by the Monterey jack cheese and the Mexican queso cheese.
9. Place under the broiler and cook for 5-10 minutes, or until cheese is melted and lightly browned.
10. Garnish with fresh cilantro before serving.

Succulent Madras Chicken Curry

Serves: 6
Preparation time: 20 minutes
Cooking time: 30 minutes

Ingredients:

6 x 4-ounce chicken breast, skinless, boneless
1 onion, diced
1 tablespoon ginger, grated
2 Thai or cayenne green chilies, minced
½ teaspoon ground cardamom
½ teaspoon ground cloves
½ teaspoon garam masala
1 teaspoon salt, black pepper
2 large tomatoes, diced
Extra virgin olive oil

Preparation:

1. Slice chicken breasts into 1" cubes.
2. Heat 4 tablespoons olive oil in cast iron deep skillet, add chicken. Brown and remove to plate.
3. In same skillet, add onion, cloves, cardamom. Sauté for a minute, add ginger, sauté for another minute.
4. Add remaining ingredients, and simmer on low for 20 minutes.
5. Serve with rice or flatbread.

Louisiana BBQ Dipping Sauce

Serve: 6
Preparation time: 5 minutes
Cooking time: 2 minutes

Ingredients:

1 small onion, minced

4 cloves garlic, minced

¾ cup tomato puree

½ cup water

¼ cup brown sugar

1 teaspoon Worcestershire

1 teaspoon salt

Preparation:

1. Heat water in cast iron sauce pot, add remaining ingredients, and bring to boil.
2. Reduce heat, simmer for 30 minutes, cool.
3. Using hand immersion blender, mix until smooth.

Chicken Pot Pie Pastry

Serves: 4-6
Preparation time: 15 minutes
Cooking time: 1hour

Ingredients:

3 cups cooked chicken breast, cubed
2 medium potatoes, peeled, diced
1 cup carrots, diced
2 tablespoons flour
1 cup half-and-half cream
½ cup milk
2 cups low-sodium chicken broth
1 onion, diced
1 teaspoon oregano
1 teaspoon thyme
1 teaspoon salt, black pepper
1 sheet puff pastry
1 egg
Extra virgin olive oil

Preparation:

1. Heat 3 tablespoons olive oil in a cast iron deep skillet, and add onions. Sauté for a minute.
2. Add carrots, potatoes, sauté for 2 minutes.
3. Mix in flour, and stir in chicken broth and spices.
4. Mix all but 2 tablespoons of milk and cream in separate bowl. Continue to mix, and slowly add in 6 tablespoons of hot chicken broth into mixture in order to raise the temperature of the milk and cream.
5. Pour creamy mixture into skillet, and mix with carrots, potatoes, bring to boil.
6. Cover pot, simmer for 20 minutes, cool.
7. Preheat oven to 425°.

8. Whisk egg with 2 tablespoons milk.
9. Roll out the puff pastry on lightly floured working area.
10. Place sheet of puff pastry over skillet. Allow pastry to hang over the sides of the skillet. Make a few vent holes to let the steam out while cooking.
11. Place into oven, and bake for 30 minutes or until pastry is a lovely golden brown color.
12. Cool and serve with a light green salad to balance the richness of the pot pie.

Turkey Pot Pie

Servings: 6
Preparation time: 20 minutes
Cooking time: 55 minutes

Ingredients:

3 cups of turkey, cooked and cubed
1 1/4 cups of cream of potato soup (1 -10.75ounce can)
1 1/4 cups of cream of chicken soup (1 -10.75ounce can)
1/2 cup of water
1/2 cup of onion, chopped
2 cups of mixed vegetables, canned (2 -15ounce cans)
1/4 teaspoon of salt
1/4 teaspoon of pepper
2 premade pie crusts

Preparation:

1. Preheat the oven to 375°F.
2. Take the premade pie crusts out of their tins. Place one in a 10" cast iron skillet. Set aside while you make the filling.
3. Place a saucepan on the stove, and set the temperature to medium-high.
4. Wash, peel, and chop the onion.
5. Mix together the turkey and onion in the saucepan.
6. Stir in the potato and chicken soup.
7. Fold in the water.
8. Add the vegetables and stir thoroughly.
9. Stir the mixture occasionally until it comes to a boil, usually about 10 minutes.
10. Reduce heat and simmer for about 5 minutes.
11. Pour the mixture into the pie shell that is in the cast iron skillet.
12. Top with the second pie crust.

13. Slice 4 or 5 slits into the top crust and crimp the edges.
14. Place in the oven, and bake for 45 minutes or until the pastry is golden brown and the mixture is bubbling.
15. Remove from heat and serve warm.

Cast Iron Turkey Burgers

Servings: 4
Preparation time: 10 minutes
Cooking time: 15 minutes

Ingredients:

1 pound of ground turkey
1/2 cup of yellow onion, chopped
1/2 cup apple sauce
1 garlic clove
2 tablespoons of butter
1 tablespoon of olive oil
1/2 teaspoon of salt
1/2 teaspoon of pepper
4 whole wheat English Muffins

Preparation:

1. Place the ground turkey and apple sauce in a bowl. Mix well. The apple sauce will keep the turkey burger moist.
2. Add the salt and pepper.
3. Place a cast iron skillet onto the stove, and pour in the oil. Set to a medium temperature, and heat the oil.
4. Mince the garlic, and place in the cast iron skillet.
5. Wash, peel, and chop the onion. Add to the cast iron skillet.
6. Sauté the onions and garlic until it is tender, about 3 to 5 minutes.
7. Add the vegetables to the turkey, and mix thoroughly.
8. Shape into balls and press a whole in the middle.
9. Add a half to 1 teaspoon dollop of butter in the center.
10. Shape the turkey ball into a patty, but make sure the butter is in the middle.
11. Place back into the hot skillet, and turn the heat up to medium-high.

12. Grill the turkey burgers until they are cooked thoroughly, usually about 3 to 4 minutes on either side.
13. While the turkey burgers are grilling, toast the English muffins.
14. Place the cooked turkey burger on top of the English muffin, garnish with your favorite toppings.
15. Serve warm.

Chicken Biryani with Mint Chutney

Serves: 4
Preparation time: 20 minutes
Cooking time: 25 minutes

Ingredients:
4 x 4 ounce chicken breasts
1 medium carrot, peeled, grated
½ head cauliflower, stemmed
1 small onion, diced
¼ cup cashews, halved
½ cup almonds, chopped
1 teaspoon curry powder
½ teaspoon cumin seeds
2 cups low-sodium organic chicken stock
1 teaspoon salt, black pepper
Coconut oil

Mint Chutney
2 cups mint, stemmed
2 dates, pitted
¼ cup coconut oil
½ cup balsamic vinegar
½ teaspoon salt
½ teaspoon black pepper

Preparation:
1. Place cauliflower in food processor, and pulse until you have small, rice-like granules, then set aside.
2. Slice chicken breast into 1" pieces.
3. Heat 4 tablespoons coconut oil in cast iron skillet
4. Add chicken breast, brown, then remove from skillet onto dish.

5. Pour another tablespoon of oil into skillet, add cumin, and toast for a 15 seconds, then add onions, carrots, cashews, and almonds, and sauté.
6. Return chicken to skillet, add curry powder, black pepper, salt, and chicken stock. Cover skillet and bring to a boil.
7. Reduce heat to medium-low, and cook for 15 minutes or until cauliflower is tender.
8. While biryani is cooking, combine ingredients for chutney in blender, mix until well-combined.
9. Serve biryani with a dollop of mint chutney and a green side salad.

Chicken Jambalaya

Serves: 6
Preparation time: 10 minutes
Cooking time: 30 minutes

Ingredients:

1 pound chicken breast
½ pound Polish sausage
1 green bell pepper, seeded, diced
1 carrot, peeled, diced
1 celery stalk, diced
1 red onion, sliced
1 head cauliflower
2 cups tomatoes, diced
2 cups low-sodium chicken stock
1 teaspoon oregano, paprika, cayenne pepper
1 teaspoon black pepper
1 teaspoon salt
1 bay leaf
Extra virgin olive oil

Preparation:

1. Chop chicken breast and Polish sausage into ½" pieces.
2. Grate cauliflower.
3. Heat 3 tablespoons extra virgin olive oil in cast iron skillet over medium heat.
4. Sauté chicken and Polish sausage for five minutes.
5. Add onion and garlic and sauté for a minute.
6. Add bell pepper, celery stalk, and carrot, and sauté for 3 minutes.
7. Add tomatoes, chicken stock, black pepper, cauliflower and spices.
8. Cover skillet and cook for 20 minutes over medium heat.
9. Serve hot.

Chicken Thighs on Artichoke Heart

Serves: 4
Preparation time: 15 minutes
Cooking time: 1hour

Ingredients:

8 chicken thighs, skinless
1 cup artichoke hearts
8 shitake mushrooms, sliced
1 red onion, sliced
2 cloves garlic
1 carrot, diced
2 tablespoons fresh dill
1 teaspoon salt
1 teaspoon black pepper
Coconut oil

Preparation:

1. Preheat oven to 375ºF.
2. Heat 4 tablespoons coconut oil in skillet, add chicken thighs, brown, and remove thighs to plate.
3. Into same skillet, add garlic and onion, and sauté for a minute.
4. Stir in shitake mushrooms, artichoke hearts, carrot, dill, salt and black pepper.
5. Place chicken thighs on vegetables, cover skillet with lid or aluminium foil, and bake in oven for 40 minutes.

Cashew-Parm Chicken

Serves: 5-6
Preparation time: Overnight +15 min.
Cooking time: 40

Ingredients:

4 x 4 ounce chicken breasts, skinless, boneless
1 cup organic tomato sauce
¾ cup cashews
4 cloves garlic, minced
1 large onion, diced
1 teaspoon oregano
1 bay leaf
1 lemon, juiced
Salt, black pepper
Coconut oil

Preparation:

1. Crush cashews in a food processor. Add lemon juice, and leave overnight.
2. Preheat oven to 375°F.
3. Heat 4 tablespoons extra virgin olive oil in cast iron skillet over medium heat.
4. Place chicken breasts in skillet, brown, remove to plate.
5. Add garlic and onions to pan, and sauté for approximately 30 seconds.
6. Add tomato sauce, chicken stock, oregano, bay leaf, salt and black pepper, and bring to boil.
7. Return chicken breast to pan, sprinkle with cashew cheese, cover with lid or aluminium paper, and bake in oven for 30 minutes.
8. Remove bay leaf before serving.

Chicken with Spinach and Raspberry Stuffing

Serves: 4
Preparation time: 25 minutes
Cooking time: 25 minutes

Ingredients:

4 x 4 ounce chicken breasts
4 slices bacon
4 cups fresh spinach, chopped
½ cup frozen or fresh raspberries
½ cup cashews, chopped
Salt, black pepper
Coconut oil

Preparation:

1. Preheat oven to 400ºF.
2. Create a slit in the side of each chicken breast, and slice in half about three-quarters of the way through.
3. Combine spinach, cashews, and a teaspoon salt and black pepper, along with 3 tablespoons coconut oil. Blend until combined but chunky.
4. Using a spoon, mix raspberries into the spinach mixture.
5. Spoon spinach into the slit part of chicken breast, wrap each breast in a slice of bacon.
6. Heat 4 tablespoons coconut oil in cast iron skillet, carefully place each breast in skillet, and brown both sides.
7. Place cast iron skillet into oven, and bake for 20 minutes.
8. Serve with Toasted Pecan and Cranberry Salad (recipe in Sides and Accompaniments).

Chicken with Asparagus Bacon Bundles

Serves: 4
Preparation time: 10 minutes
Cooking time: 45 minutes

Ingredients:
4 x 4 ounce chicken breasts
12 asparagus spears, trimmed
4 slices bacon
½ cup water
Salt, black pepper
½ teaspoon paprika
¼ cup ghee
Extra virgin olive oil

Preparation:
1. Preheat oven to 375ºF.
2. Wrap each asparagus stalk with one slice of bacon.
3. Heat ghee in cast iron skillet over medium heat, add paprika.
4. Into ghee, place chicken breasts. Brown.
5. Place asparagus bacon bundles into skillet alongside chicken.
6. Place skillet into oven, and bake for 35 minutes.

Healthy BBQ Chicken Pizza

Serves: 4
Preparation time: 15 minutes.
Cooking time: 35 minutes

Ingredients:
1 pound chicken breast
1 cup tomato puree
3 dates, pitted
½ cup cashew, chopped
1 lemon, juiced
1 clove garlic, minced
1 teaspoon oregano
1 teaspoon salt
1 teaspoon black pepper
Extra virgin olive oil

Preparation:
1. Preheat oven to 375ºF.
2. Place dates in food processor and mix into paste. Add garlic, lemon juice and tomato puree, mix, set aside.
3. Using mallet, pound chicken breasts until they are ¼" thick (or ask your butcher to do it).
4. Heat tablespoon extra virgin olive oil in skillet over medium heat, place chicken breasts in skillet so that they completely cover bottom of pan, turn over after 30 seconds.
5. Pour blender sauce over chicken, top with cashews, and slide into oven for 30 minutes.
6. Slice and serve.

Beef

Tri Colored Stuffed Pepper Casserole

Serves: 4
Preparation time: 10 minutes
Cooking time: 30 minutes

Ingredients:

1 pound ground beef
2 tablespoons olive oil
3 cloves garlic, crushed and minced
1 cup red bell pepper, diced
1 cup yellow bell pepper, diced
1 cup green bell pepper, diced
½ cup red onion, diced
¼ cup fresh basil, chopped
¼ cup parsley, chopped
1 15 ounce can crushed tomatoes, with liquid
1 cup tomato sauce
2 cups beef stock
1 tablespoon Worcestershire sauce
1 cup uncooked rice
1 teaspoon salt
1 teaspoon black pepper
1 cup provolone cheese, shredded
½ cup parmesan cheese, freshly grated

Preparation:

1. Prepare a 10- or 12-inch cast iron skillet and add the olive oil over medium heat.
2. Cook the ground beef until browned, and drain any fat.
3. Add the garlic, red bell pepper, yellow bell pepper, green bell pepper, and red onion. Sauté for 3-5 minutes.

4. Season with basil and parsley. Add the tomato sauce, beef stock and Worcestershire sauce. Stir, increase heat to medium high and bring to a boil.
5. Add the rice, salt, and black pepper. Stir, reduce heat, and cover. Simmer for 15-20 minutes, or until rice is tender.
6. Sprinkle the cheese over the rice, cover and cook an additional 5 minutes, or until cheese is melted.

Skillet Lasagna

Servings: 6
Preparation time: 10 minutes
Cooking time: 35 minutes

Ingredients:

1 pound ground beef
1 tablespoon dried basil
1 red onion
1 white onion
1 tablespoon shallot flakes
2 tablespoons dried oregano
1 box ready to use lasagna noodles
3 garlic cloves
8 cups pasta sauce
1/2 cup Parmesan cheese
2 cups mozzarella cheese, shredded

Preparation:

1. Preheat the oven to 375°F.
2. Place the ground beef into your cast iron skillet.
3. Brown the beef over medium-high temperatures until it is cooked.
4. Wash, peel and chop the red and white onions.
5. Add the onions to the beef and cook until they are fragrant and tender.
6. Drain the beef to remove a lot of the grease.
7. In a separate bowl, whisk together the pasta sauce and parmesan cheese.
8. Add the shallot flakes.
9. Mince the garlic and add to the pasta sauce, mix well.
10. Pour the pasta sauce over the meat.
11. Reduce heat to low and simmer as you prepare your lasagna.

12. Coat a large, 12 to 15 inch cast iron skillet with non-stick spray. You can also use smaller 8 inch cast iron skillets to make personal sized lasagna.
13. Pour two cups of the meat sauce into the bottom of the skillet. Spread it out so there is an even layer of sauce.
14. Separate the box of noodles into the thirds and then place 1/3 of the noodles onto the sauce in the cast iron skillet. Break the noodles as needed.
15. When the sauce is covered with noodles, spoon on another 2 cups of meat sauce.
16. Shred the mozzarella cheese.
17. Sprinkle 1/3 of the cheese over the sauce.
18. Take the second third of noodles and cover the mozzarella. Repeat until you have used all of the noodles.
19. Pour the remaining sauce onto the last layer of noodles.
20. Cover with the remaining cheese.
21. Cover the lasagna with aluminum foil and bake for 20 to 25 minutes.
22. Remove the foil and cook for another 10 minutes or until the cheese is golden.
23. Remove from the oven and allow to cool slightly before serving warm.

Cast Iron Cheeseburgers

Servings: 4
Preparation time: 10 minutes
Cooking time: 20 to 40 minutes

Ingredients:
1 1/2 pounds of ground beef
1 1/2 teaspoons of canola oil
1 teaspoon of black pepper
2 teaspoons of garlic salt
1/4 teaspoon of paprika
1/2 cup of onions
1 egg
1/4 cup of bread crumbs
4 slices of cheddar cheese
4 hamburger buns

Preparation:
1. Wash, peel, and dice the onions.
2. Place the paprika, garlic salt, and black pepper.
3. Whisk together until well blended.
4. Add the onions.
5. Place in the ground beef.
6. Carefully crack the egg into the ground beef.
7. Add the breadcrumbs.
8. Mix the ingredients by hand until the ingredients are fully mixed and the meat clings together.
9. Form the meat into 4 burgers.
10. Pour the oil into a 12" cast iron skillet.
11. Place on the stove and set the temperature to medium-high.
12. Grill the burgers for 3 to 5 minutes on each side, flipping only once, until they are cooked the way you want.
13. Slice the cheese while the burgers are cooking.

14. Place one or two slices of cheese on each burger when they are fully cooked.
15. Remove from heat.
16. Serve on a bun with your favorite toppings.

Mexican Skillet Casserole

Servings: 6
Preparation time: 10 minutes
Cooking time: 20 to 30 minutes

Ingredients:
1 pound of ground beef
2 teaspoons of canola oil
3/4 cup of salt
2 tablespoons of chili powder
4 garlic cloves
2 cups of black beans (1 -15ounce can)
1 teaspoon of cumin, ground
1 3/4 cups of onion, chopped
2 cups of diced tomatoes with jalapenos (1- 15ounce can)
1/2 cup of cheddar cheese, shredded
1 3/4 cups of white rice, cooked

Preparation:
1. Cook the rice according to the package.
2. In a 10" cast iron skillet, add the oil.
3. Place on the stove set to medium-high heat, and heat the oil.
4. Wash, peel, and chop the onion, add it to the skillet.
5. Mince the garlic, and add to the onion. Stir until it is well blended.
6. Sauté the vegetables until the onions are tender, about 3 to 5 minutes.
7. When the onions are tender, add the ground beef. Cook until it is brown, about 10 to 15 minutes.
8. Drain the beef, and return the beef to the skillet and the stove.
9. Fold in the cumin.
10. Add the salt and chili powder.

11. Stir until the ingredients are thoroughly incorporated.
12. Drain the tomatoes, and add to the beef, mix well.
13. Drain and rinse the black beans and stir until they are dispersed through the meat.
14. Fold in the rice, making sure the ingredients are well blended.
15. Cook for an additional 2 to 5 minutes or until the dish is heated.
16. Shred the cheese, and add to the top of the meat.
17. Cover with a lid, and allow to cook for another 2 minutes.
18. Remove from heat and serve warm.

Beef and Potato Pie

Servings: 6
Preparation time: 15 minutes
Cooking time: 1 hour and 20 minutes

Ingredients:
1 1/2 pounds of ground beef
1 tablespoon of canola oil
3/4 cup of beef broth
3 tablespoons of flour
1/2 teaspoon of salt
1 onion
3 red potatoes
1 egg
1 premade pie shell

Preparation:
1. Preheat the oven to 375°F.
2. Place a 10" skillet onto the stove. Set the temperature to medium high.
3. Add the oil and heat.
4. Wash, peel, and chop the onions. Add to the oil, and cook until the onions are tender, about 3 to 5 minutes.
5. Fold in the ground beef, and cook until the meat is browned, about 10 to 15 minutes.
6. While the ground beef is cooking, wash and chop the potatoes. You want about 1/2" cubes.
7. Fold the potatoes into the cooked beef, and cook for an additional minute.
8. Remove from the stove, and drain the grease from the meat.
9. Set the stove to medium-low, and return the skillet to the stove.
10. Sprinkle the beef with flour, and stir until it is fully blended.

11. Add the beef broth and mix.
12. Simmer for 2 to 3 minutes or until the sauce begins to thicken.
13. Stir in the salt and remove from heat.
14. Remove the pie shell from its aluminum plate.
15. Place the dough on top of the beef mixture.
16. Whisk the egg in a separate bowl and brush the mixture over the pie crust.
17. Cut 2 to 3 slits into the middle of the dough.
18. Place the cast iron skillet into the oven, and bake until the crust is golden brown and the mixture is bubbling, about 45 minutes.
19. Remove from oven, and let stand for 10 minutes.
20. Serve warm.

Beef Stroganoff

Servings: 6
Preparation time: 15 minutes
Cooking time: 75 minutes

Ingredients:

2 pounds of beef roast, chuck
1 onion
3 garlic cloves
1/2 cup of red wine
1 1/3 cups of beef broth
1/4 cup of all-purpose flour
4 tablespoons of butter
1/4 cup of butter
1 teaspoon of salt
1/2 teaspoon of black pepper
1 tablespoon of Worcestershire sauce
1/3 cup of sour cream
1 tablespoon of olive oil
1 teaspoon of yellow mustard
1 cup of mushrooms, sliced
1/3 cup of cream cheese
2 teaspoons of red pepper flakes, crushed

Preparation:

1. Slice the chuck roast into 1 1/2" strips.
2. Place the strips into a bowl.
3. Pour the red wine over it.
4. Add the salt and black pepper. Toss until the beef is coated. Place in the fridge and marinate for about 10 minutes. Don't overly marinate this dish.
5. After 10 minutes, remove the chuck beef, and pat dry. Do not throw away the marinade.

6. Place a cast iron skillet (a 12" skillet works best) onto the stove, and set the temperature to medium.
7. Heat the olive oil in the skillet.
8. Once the oil is hot, add the beef strips. Fry until the strips are brown, stirring occasionally. This usually takes about 5 to 7 minutes.
9. Remove the beef and set aside.
10. Drain the grease from the cast iron skillet and return it to the stove.
11. Add 2 tablespoons of butter to the skillet and melt.
12. Wash, peel, and chop the onion.
13. Mince the garlic, and add the onion and garlic to the skillet.
14. Cook until the onion is tender, about 3 to 5 minutes.
15. Once the onions are cooked, remove them, and place them in the same dish as the beef.
16. Return the skillet to the stove.
17. Add in 2 tablespoons of butter, and heat it until it melts.
18. Wash and slice the mushrooms.
19. Stir the mushrooms into the butter. Cook them until they are tender, stirring frequently, usually 7 to 10 minutes.
20. Remove the mushrooms from the heat, and place in a separate bowl. Do not add it to the beef.
21. Return the cast iron skillet to the stove.
22. Add the 1/4 cup of butter, and heat until it melts.
23. When the butter has melted, whisk in the flour. Cook for 4 minutes, stirring constantly.
24. Stir in the beef stock, and bring the butter mixture to a boil.
25. When it is boiling, reduce the heat to medium-low. Make sure that you are constantly stirring during this time or your sauce will burn.
26. Pour in the Worcestershire sauce.
27. Add the mustard.
28. Stir in the marinade that you had saved.
29. Fold in the red pepper flakes.

30. Stir until the ingredients are completely incorporated.
31. Add the beef and onion mixture.
32. Cover the skillet with a lid and simmer for 50 to 60 minutes. Cook until the meat is tender, stirring occasionally.
33. When the beef is tender, whisk together the sour cream and cream cheese until smooth.
34. Fold in the mushrooms.
35. Add the mushroom mixture to the beef mixture and cook for an additional 5 minutes.
36. Serve warm.

Greek Beef Stew

Serves: 5-6
Preparation time: 10 min.
Cooking time:

Ingredients:

2 pounds beef chuck, boneless
4 small white potatoes, cubed
1 cup carrots, sliced
1 onion, sliced
4 cups low-sodium beef stock
½ cup red wine
2 tablespoons flour
1 teaspoon oregano
Salt, black pepper
Extra virgin olive oil

Preparation:

1. Slice beef chuck into 1½" cubes, massage meat with 2 teaspoons salt and 2 teaspoons black pepper.
2. Heat 3 tablespoons extra virgin olive oil in large cast iron pot over medium heat, add beef and brown.
3. Remove beef from pot onto plate.
4. Add onions, bell pepper, and sauté until onions are translucent.
5. Mix in flour, and stir in wine.
6. Add beef stock, oregano, return beef to pot.
7. Lower heat to low
8. Add potato, carrots, cover, and simmer for an hour.

Beef and Rosemary Dumplings

Serves: 6
Preparation time: 15 minutes
Cooking time: 35 minutes

Ingredients:

2 pounds beef stew meat
¼ cup flour
1 teaspoon paprika
1 teaspoon garlic powder
1 teaspoon black pepper
1 teaspoon thyme
2 tablespoons butter
2 cloves garlic, crushed and minced
1 cup red onion, chopped
½ cup celery, diced
2 cups beef stock
1 cup apple cider
1 cup carrots, chopped
1 cup fresh peas
1 cup parsnips, chopped
¼ cup flour
¼ cup seasoned bread crumbs
2 tablespoons vegetable shortening
1 tablespoon fresh rosemary, chopped
1 teaspoon fresh dill, chopped
½ teaspoon salt
½ teaspoon black pepper
1 egg, beaten

Preparation:

1. In a bowl combine ¼ cup flour, paprika, garlic powder, black pepper and thyme. Toss the stew meat pieces into the seasoned flour to coat. Set aside.
2. Prepare a 12-inch cast iron skillet and heat the butter over medium heat. Add the garlic, red onion, and celery. Sauté for 2-3 minutes.
3. Add the beef and cook until browned, approximately 5 minutes.
4. Add the beef stock and apple cider, scraping the pan. Increase the heat to medium high and bring to a boil.
5. Reduce heat to medium low and add the carrots, peas, and parsnips. Cover and simmer for approximately 45 minutes.
6. While stew is cooking, combine ¼ cup flour, bread crumbs, vegetable shortening, rosemary, dill, salt, black pepper, and egg. Mix until a dough forms. Using tablespoon sized mounds, form the dough into rough ball-shaped dumplings.
7. Place the dumplings in the stew and cook an additional 15 minutes before serving.

Mole Chile and Cornbread

Serves: 6
Preparation time: 15 minutes
Cooking time: 45 minutes

Ingredients:

1 pound ground beef
4 cloves garlic, crushed and minced
2 cups black beans (canned or precooked)
1 cup kidney beans (canned or precooked)
1 15 ounce can fire roasted tomatoes
2 cups fresh corn kernels
4 cups beef stock
2 tablespoons tomato paste
2 tablespoons unsweetened cocoa powder
¼ cup smoked paprika
1 tablespoon ancho chili powder
1 teaspoon cinnamon
1 teaspoon salt
1 teaspoon black pepper
1 cup cornmeal mix
1 egg, beaten
¼ cup vegetable oil
¾ cup whole milk
1 cup cheddar cheese, shredded
Scallions for garnish

Preparation:
1. Preheat the oven to 425°F.
2. Prepare a 12-inch deep cast iron skillet and add the ground beef and garlic. Cook over medium heat for 5-7 minutes, or until browned. Drain off any residual grease from the meat.
3. Add the black beans, kidney beans, fire roasted tomatoes and corn. Stir to mix.
4. Gently push the ingredients to the outside perimeter of the skillet. To the center add the beef stock, tomato paste, cocoa powder, smoked paprika, ancho chili powder, and cinnamon.
5. Stir the center to mix the seasonings together and then begin to incorporate the rest of the ingredients, eventually mixing everything together throughout the entire skillet. Season with salt and black pepper as desired.
6. Reduce heat to low and let simmer while the cornbread topping is prepared.
7. In a bowl, combine the cornmeal mix, egg, vegetable oil, whole milk, and cheddar cheese. Pour the mixture over the chili and spread, starting in the center and spreading out toward the edges of the pan.
8. Place in the oven and bake for 25-30 minutes, or until the top is golden brown.
9. Garnish with scallions before serving.

Italian Beef and Tomatoes

Serves: 4
Preparation time: 10 minutes
Cooking time: 25 minutes

Ingredients:

2 pounds choice beef steak, approximately 1½ inch in thickness
¼ cup olive oil, divided
5 cloves garlic, crushed and minced
4 cups mini tomatoes of various colors, halved
3 cups fresh spinach, torn
1 sprig fresh rosemary
1 tablespoon fresh thyme
½ cup fresh basil, chopped
1 teaspoon sea salt
1 teaspoon ground black peppercorns
3 tablespoons olive oil, divided

Preparation:

1. Preheat oven to 375°F.
2. Prepare a 12-inch cast iron skillet and heat two tablespoons of the olive oil over medium high heat.
3. Add the garlic and sauté for 1 minute. Add the tomatoes and sauté for 2 minutes before adding the spinach. Cook for an additional 1-2 minutes, or until spinach is lightly wilted. Remove contents with a slotted spoon and set aside.
4. Add the remaining oil to the skillet. Once the oil is hot, add the steaks and season with salt and ground black peppercorns. Sear the steaks on each side, until brown, approximately 7 minutes per side.
5. Add the tomatoes and spinach back into the pan. Season with rosemary, thyme and basil. Place the skillet into the oven and bake until steak reaches desired doneness, approximately 6-10 minutes.
6. Let rest 10 minutes before serving.

Spaghetti and Meatballs

Serves: 4
Preparation time: 15 minutes.
Cooking time: 35 minutes

Ingredients:

1 pound ground beef
¾ cup bread, cubed
1 teaspoon garlic, minced
1 small onion, minced
1 tablespoon tomato paste
4 cups tomato puree
1 cup chicken stock
3 fresh basil leaves
1 teaspoon oregano
1 teaspoon salt, black pepper
1/2 package spaghetti noodles

Preparation:

1. Place a large pot of salted water to boil.
2. Add spaghetti to boiling water approximately 10 minutes before serving dish, cook according to package instructions.
3. Combine ground beef, bread, garlic, onion, tomato paste, oregano, salt, black pepper in bowl.
4. Using hands, shape 1" meatballs.
5. Heat 4 tablespoons olive oil in skillet.
6. Place meatballs in large cast iron skillet, and cook for seven minutes. Ensure all sides are browned and cooked.
7. Add tomato puree and chicken stock to skillet, simmer on low for 20 minutes.
8. Add basil, simmer for another 5 minutes.
9. Serve spaghetti with meatballs.

Deep Dish Beef Lovers Pizza

Serves: 4-6
Preparation time: 15 minutes
Cooking time: 30 minutes

Ingredients:

1 pound flank steak, sliced into thin strips
2 cloves garlic, crushed and minced
¼ cup shallots, sliced
2 cups portabella mushrooms, sliced
1 teaspoon crushed red pepper flakes
1 teaspoon salt
1 teaspoon black pepper
2 tablespoons olive oil, divided
1 ball premade pizza dough, enough for one large pizza
1 cup canned fire roasted tomatoes, drained
1 cup heirloom tomatoes, sliced
½ cup smoked Gouda, cut into very small cubes
1 cup fresh mozzarella, shredded
½ cup parmesan, freshly grated

Preparation:

1. Preheat oven to 425°F.
2. Prepare a 12-inch cast iron skillet and heat 1 tablespoon of the olive oil over medium heat.
3. Add the steak strips, garlic, and shallots. Cook, stirring, for approximately 5 minutes, or until steak has almost reached desired doneness. Add the mushrooms, red pepper flakes, salt, and black pepper and sauté an additional 2 minutes.
4. Using a slotted spoon, remove the contents and set aside. Let skillet cool enough to be handled.

5. Roll out the dough into a large circle at least 14 inches in diameter. Press the dough directly into the pan, on top of any pan drippings that remained. Spread the dough along the bottom of the skillet and up along the sides.
6. Brush the dough with the remaining olive oil and add a layer of the heirloom tomatoes. Next add the beef and mushroom mixture, followed by the Gouda cheese.
7. Add the fire roasted tomatoes and spread them as evenly over the top as possible. Top with mozzarella and then parmesan cheese.
8. Place the skillet over medium heat and cook for 3-5 minutes before placing in the oven and baking 15-20 minutes or until crust is golden brown and cheese is bubbly.
9. Let rest slightly before serving.

Orange Ginger Beef on Egg Noodle Bed

Serves: 4
Preparation time: 20 minutes
Cooking time: 15 minutes

Ingredients:
16 ounces flank steak, thinly sliced
2 teaspoons fresh ginger, grated
½ cup fresh orange juice
¼ cup soy sauce
1 teaspoon salt, black pepper
Extra virgin olive oil

1 pkg (400-450g) egg noodles

Preparation:
1. Heat 3 tablespoons extra virgin olive oil in a cast iron deep skillet over medium-high heat. Add steak, brown for a minute.
2. Stir in remaining ingredients, and reduce heat to low. Cook for 10 minutes.
3. Cook egg noodles according to directions on package, drain.
4. Serve Orange Ginger Beef on Egg Noodle bed.

Simply Delicious Beef Chili

Serves: 4
Preparation time: 15 minutes
Cooking time: 1 hour

Ingredients:
1 pound stewing beef
Olive or coconut oil for cooking
1 cup red kidney beans
1 medium onion, diced
4 cloves garlic, minced
4 cups crushed tomatoes
3 cups beef stock
1 teaspoon cumin
1 teaspoon oregano
1 teaspoon paprika
1 teaspoon salt, black pepper

Preparation:
1. Place the beef in the freezer for 15 minutes. With a sharp knife, cut the beef into small bite-sized cubes. Pat dry the meat with kitchen paper towels.
2. Heat 3 tablespoons olive oil in cast iron deep skillet over medium-high heat. Add beef without overcrowding it. You may need to cook it in a few batches. Brown the beef on every side.
3. Remove beef from pot to plate.
4. Into same pot add onion and garlic. Sauté (add a little more oil if necessary).
5. Add crush tomatoes, and simmer for 5 minutes on medium-low.
6. Return beef to pot, add remaining ingredients, and reduce heat to medium-low.
7. Cook for 45 minutes, stirring throughout cooking process.
8. Serve beef chili with a nice toasty bun.

Delicious Pan Quesadillas

Serves: 6
Preparation time: 25 minutes
Cooking time: 25 minutes

Ingredients:
2 cups salsa
1 pound lean ground beef
1 onion, diced
4 cloves garlic, minced
1 avocado, pitted, peeled, thinly sliced
1 lime, juiced
½ teaspoon salt
2 cups salsa
2 cups sour cream
4 tortillas
Extra virgin olive oil

Side Salad
2 cups iceberg lettuce, shredded
1 small onion, sliced
1 tomato, diced
Sour cream
Salsa

Preparation:
1. Heat 3 tablespoons olive oil in cast iron deep skillet, add ground beef, onions, garlic, and sauté until beef has browned. Remove mixture to plate.
2. In same skillet, spread 3 tablespoons salsa, next layer tortilla, top with a half of beef mixture, sprinkle with cheese, layer next tortilla, spread tortilla with a little sour cream, sprinkle with cheese, and top with avocado slices.

3. Place next layer of tortilla, spread salsa on tortilla, place remaining half of beef on tortilla, sprinkle with cheese.
4. Top with remaining tortilla, spread top with sour cream, and sprinkle with cheese.
5. Place skillet on stove over low heat, cover, and cook for 10 minutes.
6. Remove lid, increase heat to medium, and cook for another few minutes until moisture from bottom of pan has evaporated. Cool quesadillas, slice into eighths.
7. Toss together lettuce, tomato, onion and serve mixture with a dollop of sour cream and salsa alongside quesadilla.

Rich Heritage Lasagna

Serves: 4
Preparation time: 10 minutes
Cooking time: 30 minutes

Ingredients:
1 tablespoon olive oil
1 cup red onion, diced
½ cup red bell pepper
4 cloves garlic, crushed and minced
1 pound ground beef, crumbled
½ cup fresh basil, chopped
1 tablespoon fresh oregano, chopped
1 teaspoon salt
1 teaspoon black pepper
4 cups fire roasted canned tomatoes, with liquid
10 lasagna noodles, broken into 2-3 inch pieces
1 cup fresh mozzarella cheese, shredded
1 cup ricotta cheese
½ cup parmesan cheese

Preparation:
1. Preheat broiler.
2. Prepare a 12-inch cast iron skillet and heat the olive oil over medium heat.
3. Add the ground beef and cook until browned, approximately 7 minutes. Drain any fat.
4. Add the red onion, bell pepper, and garlic. Cook while stirring until onion and pepper are slightly tender, approximately 3 minutes.
5. Season with basil, oregano, salt and black pepper. Add in the tomatoes and increase heat to medium high. Bring to a low boil, add the lasagna noodles, stir and reduce heat to a simmer. Cook for 10 minutes.

6. In a bowl, combine the mozzarella cheese, ricotta cheese and parmesan cheese. Mix well.
7. Place spoonfuls of the cheese mixture around the skillet.
8. Place the skillet under the broiler for 5-7 minutes, or until cheese is lightly browned.
9. Let cool slightly before serving.

All in One Hamburger Casserole

Serves: 4
Preparation time: 10 minutes
Cooking time: 20 minutes

Ingredients:
1 pound ground beef
1 cup red onion, diced
2 cups tomatoes, diced
¼ cup ketchup
¼ cup yellow mustard
¼ Worcestershire sauce
¼ cup dill pickles, diced
1 tablespoon vegetable oil
4 cups shredded potatoes, moisture removed
1 teaspoon garlic powder
1 teaspoon oregano
1 teaspoon salt
1 teaspoon black pepper
1 cup cheddar cheese, shredded

Preparation:
1. Prepare a 12-inch skillet and add the ground beef over medium heat. Cook until lightly browned, 4-5 minutes. Drain any fat.
2. Add the red onion and tomatoes. Cook for 3-4 minutes. Season with ketchup, yellow mustard, Worcestershire sauce and dill pickles. Mix well. Remove from the skillet and set aside.
3. Add the vegetable oil to the pan and increase heat to medium high. Add the shredded potatoes. Cook, while tossing, for 3 minutes. Season with garlic powder, oregano, salt, and black pepper. Press the potatoes into

the pan and cook for 5 minutes, or until bottom becomes crispy.

4. Add the ground beef back into the skillet and toss with the potatoes. Cook for an additional 3-5 minutes, or until heated through.

5. Top with shredded cheddar cheese before serving.

Green Chile Tamale Pie

Servings: 4
Preparation time: 15 minutes
Cooking time: 1 hour and 20 minutes

Ingredients:

1 cup of ground beef
1 cup of masa harina
1 cup of lima beans
1 cup of boiling water
3 garlic cloves
1 poblano chili
1/4 teaspoon of ground red pepper
1/2 teaspoon of black pepper
1 teaspoon of salt
1 tablespoon of olive oil
8 small tomatillos
2 tablespoons of butter
1/4 cup of crumbled queso fresco
1 lime
2 tablespoons of fresh cilantro
1/2 teaspoon of baking powder

Preparation:

1. Preheat oven to 400°F.
2. In a large bowl, mix together the ground red pepper and 1/4 teaspoon of salt.
3. Add the masa harina and mix thoroughly.
4. Create a well in the spices.
5. Pour in the boiling water.
6. Mix until you have a soft dough. Cover and set aside.
7. Place a 9" cast iron skillet onto the stove. Set the temperature to medium-high.
8. Add the olive oil.

9. Place the ground beef in the skillet, and cook until it is browned. Usually about 10 to 15 minutes.
10. Wash, peel, and chop onion. Add it to the skillet.
11. Mince the garlic, and add to the beef.
12. Wash, seed, and chop the poblano pepper.
13. Add the pepper, black pepper, and the remaining salt to the skillet.
14. Continue to cook until the onion is tender, about 5 minutes.
15. Add the tomatillos.
16. Rinse the lima beans, and add them to the beef. Continue to cook for 2 minutes.
17. Remove from the heat, and set to the side.
18. Take the masa mixture, and add the baking powder.
19. Fold in the butter, and mix until smooth.
20. Spread the masa batter over the filling in the skillet.
21. Cover the skillet with an oven-safe lid.
22. Place in the oven, and bake for 30 minutes.
23. Uncover and bake for an additional 10 minutes. The crust should be lightly browned on the edges.
24. Remove from oven.
25. Slice the lime into wedges, and serve with the pie as a garnish.
26. Serve warm.

Cast Iron Roast Beef

Servings: 6
Preparation time: 20 minutes
Cooking time: 2 hours and 20 minutes

Ingredients:
1 beef roast (best is a Prime Rib roast that is 4.5 pounds)
1/4 cup of butter, unsalted
1 teaspoon of black pepper
1 teaspoon of coarse sea salt
1 onion
4 sprigs of fresh thyme
1/4 cup of red wine
1 onion
4 cups of beef stock

Preparation:
1. Preheat oven to 275°F.
2. In a small bowl, whisk together the salt and the pepper.
3. Rub the pepper mixture onto the roast.
4. Place a 12" cast iron skillet onto the stove that is set to medium-high.
5. Set the roast in the pan, and sear the meat. What this means is that you turn the meat in the pan so that every side of the roast has been cooked slightly. Generally, you should sear the meat for 2 to 3 minutes per side.
6. Once the meat is seared, transfer the skillet to the oven. Bake for 45 minutes.
7. Wash and peel the onions.
8. Cut the onion into quarters.
9. Remove the roast from the oven, and sprinkle the onion around the roast.

10. Return to the oven, and continue cooking for 1½ to 2 hours. You want the internal temperature, at the thickest spot on the roast, to reach 130°F. Use a meat thermometer for best results.
11. Remove the roast, and carefully wrap it in aluminum foil.
12. Return just the roast to the oven for 15 to 20 minutes.
13. While it is in the oven, pour the drippings in the skillet into a bowl.
14. Using a spoon, remove the fat from the top of the drippings.
15. Return the drippings to the skillet, and place the skillet onto the stove with the temperature set at medium.
16. Fold in the onions.
17. Add the butter, and heat until it melts.
18. Whisk in the flour, and stir for about 2 minutes until you have a paste.
19. Pour in the red wine, and mix until it is smooth.
20. Add the beef stock, and mix thoroughly.
21. Finally, wash and add the thyme sprigs.
22. Bring the ingredients to a boil, and then reduce the heat to low.
23. Simmer for 5 to 8 minutes, stirring constantly, or until the gravy has thickened.
24. Remove the onions and thyme, and throw them away.
25. Remove the roast from the oven.
26. Slice and serve with the gravy and a favorite side.

Creamy Basil Flank Steak

Serves: 4
Preparation time: 10 minutes
Cooking time: 30 minutes

Ingredients:

2 pounds flank steak, pounded to even thickness
1 tablespoon vegetable oil
3 cloves garlic, crushed and minced
1 teaspoon Worcestershire sauce
1 teaspoon salt
1 teaspoon black pepper
4 cups green beans, washed and trimmed
½ cup beef broth
1 teaspoon cornstarch
2 teaspoons ground black peppercorns
¼ cup fresh basil, chopped
1 tablespoon chives, chopped
½ teaspoon salt
½ cup cream cheese, softened

Preparation:

1. Prepare a 12-inch cast iron skillet and heat the vegetable oil over medium high heat.
2. Place the steak in the pan and season with garlic, Worcestershire sauce, salt, and black pepper. Sear on both sides until browned, approximately 10 minutes per side. Remove the steak from the pan and set aside to rest.
3. Meanwhile, add the green beans to the pan and sauté in the meat juices just until color brightens, approximately 3-4 minutes. Remove and set aside with the steak.
4. In a small bowl combine the beef broth and cornstarch. Whisk until smooth and add to the hot skillet.

5. Season with black peppercorns, basil, chives and salt. Mix well.
6. Add the cream cheese and whisk in the pan until the cheese has broken up and blended smoothly with the broth. Cook for 1-2 minutes.
7. Serve the warm basil sauce over the steak with the green beans on the side.

The Best Beef Sliders

Serves: 5-6
Preparation time: 25 minutes
Cooking time: 7 minutes

Ingredients:
2 pounds ground beef
2 large onions, thinly-sliced
1 tablespoon Worcestershire sauce
3 tablespoons flour
1 teaspoon salt, black pepper
16 buns
Extra virgin olive oil

Topping ingredients
Dill pickles

Preparation:
1. Combine ground beef, Worcestershire sauce, salt, black pepper, flour in bowl.
2. Divide beef evenly into 16 meatballs (approx. 1¾").
3. Heat 1 tablespoon oil in large cast iron skillet, add onions, and cook for a minute.
4. Sprinkle a little water into skillet to create steam.
5. Place approximately 6 slider balls on top of onion, and using spatula, press down to form patties.
6. Place bun halves on top of each slider, which will allow steam to cook through slider and warm bun at the same time.
7. Cook for approximately 5 minutes (do not turn over).
8. Serve topped with dill pickles.

Korean Spiced Beef and Jasmine Rice

Serves: 4
Preparation time: 10 minutes
Cooking time: 20 minutes

Ingredients:
2 tablespoons vegetable oil
1 pound beef steak, cut into thin strips
¼ cup soy sauce
2 tablespoons brown sugar
1 tablespoon honey
1 tablespoon sesame seeds
2 teaspoons sesame oil
2 teaspoons garlic paste
2 cloves garlic, crushed and minced
1 cup yellow onion, sliced
1 cup savoy cabbage, shredded
2 cups broccoli florets
1 cup carrots, sliced thin
4 cups jasmine rice, cooked
Scallions, sliced for garnish

Preparation:
1. Prepare a 10- or 12-inch cast iron skillet and add the vegetable oil over medium high heat. Add the steak and sauté for 2-3 minutes, or until browned. Push meat to the outer edges of the skillet.
2. To the center of the skillet add the soy sauce, brown sugar, honey, sesame seeds, sesame oil, and garlic paste. Stir until fragrant, approximately 1 minute.
3. Add the garlic and onion. Sauté for 2 minutes.
4. Add the savoy cabbage, broccoli and carrots. Sauté for 3 minutes before introducing the meat back into the center of the pan.
5. Stir in the jasmine rice right before serving.
6. Garnish with fresh scallions.

110

Mexicasa Beef Tacos

Serves: 6
Preparation time: 10 minutes
Cooking time: 10 minutes

Ingredients:
2 pounds ground beef
1 onion, diced
1 tomato, diced
4 cloves garlic, minced
1 teaspoon oregano
1 teaspoon cumin
1 teaspoon paprika
1 teaspoon salt, black pepper
12 taco shells hard or soft
Extra virgin olive oil

Topping ingredients
½ cup cheddar cheese, grated
1 cup lettuce, shredded
1 cup salsa
1 cup sour cream

Preparation:
1. Heat 3 tablespoons olive oil in medium cast iron skillet.
2. Add garlic, onion, tomato, sauté for a minute.
3. Add ground beef, brown.
4. Add spices, mix well, cook for 5 minutes, and remove from heat.
5. Scoop beef mixture into heated taco shells, top with lettuce, sour cream, salsa, cheese, and serve.

Red Beef Curry

Serves: 4-6
Preparation time: 10 minutes
Cooking time: 30 minutes

Ingredients:
16 ounces sirloin steak
1 red bell pepper, seeded, diced
1 medium carrot, peeled, grated
1 medium onion, diced
¼ cup cashews, halved
1 tablespoon tomato paste
½ teaspoon turmeric
¼ teaspoon cinnamon
1 teaspoon curry powder
2 cups low-sodium organic chicken stock
1 cup coconut milk
1 teaspoon salt, black pepper
Coconut oil

Preparation:
1. Slice steak against the grain into ½" wide strips.
2. Heat 4 tablespoons coconut oil in cast iron skillet over medium-high heat, add steak and sauté for two minutes, remove from pan.
3. Add a little more coconut oil to pan if necessary, add onion, garlic, and give a quick sauté until garlic is fragrant.
4. Add carrot, bell pepper, and cashews, and sauté for another minute.
5. Mix in tomato paste, turmeric, cinnamon, curry powder.
6. Add in coconut milk, chicken stock, salt, and black pepper, and cover skillet and bring to simmer.
7. Reduce heat to low. and cook for 20 minutes.
8. Serve Red Beef Curry with Cauliflower Rice.

Pancetta Meatballs with Red Bell Slaw

Serves: 24 meatballs
Preparation time: 15 minutes
Cooking time: 25 minutes

Ingredients:

1 pound lean ground beef
½ pound Pancetta, chopped
1 small onion, minced
4 cloves garlic, minced
1 large onion, sliced
1 tablespoon coconut flour
1 egg
3 red bell peppers, seeded, julienned
1 lemon, juiced
½ teaspoon oregano
Salt and pepper
Extra light olive oil

Preparation:

1. Preheat oven to 400ºF.
2. Crack egg into large bowl and whisk.
3. Add ground beef, pancetta, minced onion, garlic, coconut flour, oregano, 1 teaspoon salt, and 1 teaspoon black pepper, and combine.
4. Roll into 1" meatballs.
5. Heat 4 tablespoons extra virgin olive oil in cast iron skillet.
6. Place meatballs in skillet, brown, and slide skillet into oven for 15 minutes.
7. Combine bell peppers, onions with 5 tablespoons extra virgin olive oil, lemon, salt, black pepper to taste.
8. Serve meatballs with bell pepper and onion slaw.

Beef Ragu

Serves: 4
Preparation time: 20 minutes
Cooking time: 30 minutes

Ingredients:

1 pound stewing beef, cubed
1 celery stalk, diced
1 onion, diced
2 carrots, diced
1 cup tomatoes, diced
8 cloves garlic, minced
2 cups chicken stock
1 teaspoon rosemary
1 teaspoon salt
1 teaspoon black pepper
Extra virgin olive oil

Preparation:

1. Preheat oven to 350ºF.
2. Heat 5 tablespoons extra virgin olive oil in cast iron skillet over medium-high heat.
3. Add beef and brown.
4. Reduce heat to medium-low add onion and garlic, and sauté for a minute.
5. Stir in carrots, celery, rosemary, salt, and black pepper, and cook for 5 minutes.
6. Add chicken stock and tomato, and cover.
7. Place cast iron skillet in oven, and cook for 2 hours.
8. Serve Beef Ragu over ZuCa Noodles (recipe in Vegetarian and Side category).

Beef and Sweet Potato Casserole

Serves: 5-6
Preparation time: 15 minutes
Cooking time: 45 minutes

Ingredients:
1 pound ground beef
3 sweet potatoes
1 medium onion, sliced
½ cup cashews
1 cup coconut milk
½ teaspoon thyme
Salt and black pepper
Extra virgin olive oil

Preparation:
1. Preheat oven to 375°F.
2. Peel sweet potatoes and slice into ½" rounds.
3. Place 4 tablespoons extra virgin olive oil in skillet, and heat over medium-high heat.
4. Add onion and garlic, and sauté for 30 seconds.
5. Add beef and brown. Stir in 1 teaspoon salt and thyme, remove from heat.
6. Top beef with sweet potato slices, sprinkle with ½ teaspoon salt, black pepper.
7. Cover potatoes with coconut milk and sprinkle cashews. Cover with lid or aluminum foil.
8. Bake casserole in oven for 40 minutes.
9. Cool for 10 minutes before serving.

Succulent Steak Salad with Sweet Potato

Serves: 6
Preparation time: 15 minutes
Cooking time: 30 minutes

Ingredients:
2 x 8 ounce top sirloin steak
12 cherry tomatoes, halved
1 English cucumber, sliced
2 cups arugula, chopped
1 cup green lettuce, chopped
1 large sweet potato
1 teaspoon salt
1 teaspoon black pepper
Extra light olive oil

Preparation:
1. Slice sweet potatoes into ½"-thick rounds.
2. Heat 3 tablespoons extra virgin olive oil in cast iron skillet.
3. Cook sweet potatoes approximately 8 minutes per side or until tender, and remove to plate.
4. Into same cast iron skillet place top sirloin steaks, cook 5-6 minutes per side for medium-rare, remove to plate.
5. In a large bowl combine arugula, lettuce, cucumbers, tomato.
6. Evenly divide salad among four plates. Place a few potato discs per plate.
7. Slice top sirloin against the grain into ¼" slices and place atop the salad.
8. Top with Paleo Ranch Dressing (recipe in Sides and Condiments) and serve.

Mini Eggplant Lasagna

Serves: 4
Preparation time: 10 minutes
Cooking time: 50 minutes

Ingredients:
1 pound lean ground beef
4 Chinese eggplants
1 medium onion, diced
4 cloves garlic
2 cups tomato puree
1 lemon, juiced
1 teaspoon black pepper
1 teaspoon salt
Extra light olive oil

Preparation:
1. Preheat oven to 400ºF.
2. Slice eggplant in half horizontally and in half again vertically.
3. Heat 4 tablespoons extra virgin olive oil in cast iron skillet.
4. Add ground beef, brown, remove to plate.
5. Add garlic, onion, sauté.
6. Pour tomato puree into skillet, mix.
7. Set eggplant in skillet flesh-side up.
8. Spoon beef onto flesh of each eggplant, ladle some of the tomato puree on top of eggplant.
9. Cover skillet and bake in oven for 40 minutes.

Pork and Lamb

Creamed Corn and Bacon Skillet

Servings: 6
Preparation time: 15 minutes
Cooking time: 1 hour and 20 minutes

Ingredients:

6 ears of corn

4 slices of bacon

2 cups of milk

1 cup of leeks, chopped

1 teaspoon of sugar

1 tablespoon of cornstarch

1/2 teaspoon of salt

1/4 teaspoon of black pepper

Preparation:

1. Fill a large pot with water, and set on a stove. Set the temperature to high.
2. Bring to a boil.
3. Husk and wash the corn. When the water comes to a boil, add the corn.
4. Cook until you have the desired consistency. This will probably be different for everyone. If you like a softer corn, leave it in for longer. Corn is ready in 3 to 10 minutes.
5. Once it is cooked, remove from the heat and cool completely.
6. Using a knife, cut the kernels from the corn. You want about 3 cups.
7. Scrape the corn cobs so you get the remaining pulp from the corn.
8. Add the corn scrapes to a food processor.

9. Pour in 1 1/2 cups of the corn kernels.
10. Add in the milk.
11. Combine the salt, sugar, pepper, and cornstarch. Add to the food processor.
12. Blend the ingredients in the food processor until it is smooth, about 5 minutes.
13. Place a 12" cast iron skillet onto the stove, and set the temperature to medium-heat.
14. Add the bacon and cook until the bacon is crisp, about 3 to 5 minutes.
15. Remove the bacon, and also reserve 1 teaspoon of drippings.
16. Crumble the bacon, drain the pan, and place the 1 teaspoon of drippings back into it.
17. Set back on the stove.
18. Wash and chop the leeks.
19. Add to the bacon drippings.
20. Cook the leeks until they are tender, about 2 to 3 minutes.
21. When they are tender, pour in the corn mixture from the food processor.
22. Fold in the remaining corn kernels.
23. Bring the ingredients to a boil, stirring constantly. This usually takes about 5 minutes.
24. Once it is boiling, reduce heat to low. Simmer until the mixture is thick and creamy, usually about 3 minutes.
25. Remove from heat, sprinkle with the bacon.
26. Serve warm.

Pork Chops with Pepper Jelly Sauce

Servings: 4
Preparation time: 15 minutes
Cooking time: 40 minutes

Ingredients:
2 1/4 pounds of pork loin, bone-in (4 -3/4" thick chops)
3 tablespoons of butter
3 tablespoons of olive oil
1/3 cup of white wine
1/2 cup of red pepper jelly
1 tablespoon of flour, all purpose
1 teaspoon of salt
3/4 teaspoon of black pepper
1 jalapeno pepper
1 cup of chicken broth

Preparation:
1. In a small bowl, whisk together the salt and pepper.
2. Sprinkle over the pork and rub it into the meat.
3. Place a 12" cast iron skillet on the stove. Set heat to medium-high.
4. Add 3 tablespoons of oil and 1 tablespoon of butter to the skillet. Heat until the butter is melted.
5. Place the pork chops into the skillet and grill until fully cooked. This should be about 8 minutes on one side and 10 minutes on the other.
6. After the pork chops are cooked, remove from the heat, but keep them warm in the oven.
7. Wash, seed, and chop the jalapeno.
8. Toss the jalapeno in the flour, and add to the skillet.
9. Cook until the jalapenos are golden brown, about 2 to 3 minutes.

10. Pour in the wine and stir, making sure you scrape the bottom of the pan. Cook until the wine is almost reduced, about 2 minutes.
11. Stir in the chicken broth, and cook until it begins to thicken, about 2 to 3 minutes.
12. Add the pepper jelly and continue to cook until the ingredients are thick, about 3 to 4 minutes.
13. Remove the skillet from the heat, and add the remaining butter, stirring until it has melted.
14. Place the pork chops into the sauce, and turn until they are coated.
15. Serve warm with sauce.

Cider Baked Pork and Apple

Serves: 6
Preparation time: 10 minutes
Cooking time: 45 minutes

Ingredients:
2-3 pounds pork tenderloin roast
¼ cup olive oil, divided
1 cup sweet yellow onions, sliced
3 cloves garlic, crushed and minced
1 teaspoon crushed red pepper flakes
1 teaspoon paprika
1 teaspoon thyme
1 cup apple cider
3 cups red baking apples, cut into wedges
3 cups sweet potatoes, cubed
½ teaspoon nutmeg
½ teaspoon coriander
1 teaspoon salt
1 teaspoon black pepper

Preparation:
1. Preheat oven to 425°F.
2. Prepare a 12-inch cast iron skillet and 2 tablespoons of the olive oil. Heat over medium.
3. Add the onion, and garlic. Sauté for 2-3 minutes.
4. Season the tenderloin with crushed red pepper flakes, paprika, and thyme. Place the tenderloin in the skillet and brown evenly on all sides, approximately 2-3 minutes per side. Pour in the apple cider and reduce heat to simmer.
5. Meanwhile, combine the baking apples and sweet potatoes in a bowl. Drizzle with the remaining olive oil and season with nutmeg, coriander, salt, and black pepper. Toss to coat.

6. Add the vegetables to the skillet with the pork. Remove the skillet from the heat and place in the oven. Bake for 30-35 minutes, or until internal temperature measures 160°F.
7. Let rest 10 minutes before serving.

Bright and Early Sausage Potato Hash

Serves: 4-6
Preparation time: 10 minutes
Cooking time: 20 minutes

Ingredients:
1 pound pork breakfast sausage, crumbled
½ cup yellow onion, diced
2 cups potatoes, shredded and patted dry to remove excess moisture
1 teaspoon garlic powder
½ teaspoon thyme
1 teaspoon salt
1 teaspoon black pepper
6 eggs
1 cup mild cheddar cheese, shredded
Scallions, sliced for garnish

Preparation:
1. Preheat broiler.
2. Prepare a 12-inch cast iron skillet and add the breakfast sausage. Brown over medium heat for approximately 5 minutes. Drain the fat.
3. Add the shredded potatoes and onion. Toss with cooked sausage. Season with garlic powder, thyme, salt, and black pepper.
4. Using the back of a wooden spoon, firmly press the sausage and potato mixture into the bottom of the pan, creating a firm layer. Increase the heat to medium high and cook for 3-5 minutes without stirring.
5. Lift the crust gently to check for brownness and crispness. Once a nice crispy texture has developed, gently flip the potatoes over and cook for an additional 3 minutes.

6. Crack the eggs over the potato and sausage crust and top with shredded mild cheddar cheese.
7. Remove the skillet from the heat and place it under the broiler for 5-7 minutes, or until eggs have reached desired doneness.
8. Garnish with fresh scallions before serving.

Big Ranch Chops and Vegetables

Serves: 4
Preparation time: 10 minutes
Cooking time: 35 minutes

Ingredients:

4 pork chops, bone-in, about 8 ounces. each, ¾ to 1-inch thick
2 tablespoons olive oil
4 cups small red potatoes, halved
4 cups green beans, washed and trimmed
1 tablespoon fresh dill, chopped
½ cup fresh parsley, chopped
4 cloves garlic, crushed and minced
1 teaspoon paprika
1 teaspoon salt
1 teaspoon black pepper

Preparation:

1. Preheat oven to 400°F.
2. Prepare a 12-inch cast iron skillet and brush with olive oil. Place the pork chops in the pan.
3. In a bowl, combine the potatoes and green beans. Drizzle with remaining olive oil and toss to coat. Add the vegetables to the pan with the pork chops.
4. Season with dill, parsley, garlic, paprika, salt, and black pepper. Place the skillet in the oven and bake for 30-35 minutes, or until potatoes are tender and pork chops are cooked through.

Grilled Pork Quesadillas

Servings: 4
Preparation time: 5 minutes
Cooking time: 10 minutes

Ingredients:
1/2 pound of barbecued pork, shredded
5 green onions
1/2 cup of barbecue sauce
1 cup of cheddar cheese
1/4 cup of fresh cilantro
2 tablespoons of butter
8 flour tortillas (6")

Preparation:
1. Place the barbecued pork in a bowl.
2. Wash, peel, and mince the green onions.
3. Add the barbecue sauce and green onions to the pork. Mix well.
4. Wash and chop the cilantro. Add to the pork.
5. Mix until the ingredients are fully incorporated.
6. Place a 10" cast iron skillet onto the stove and set the heat to medium.
7. Butter one side of a whole tortilla.
8. Place in the skillet, and add about 3 to 4 tablespoons to half of the tortilla, more if the tortilla can be filled.
9. Sprinkle 2 to 3 tablespoons of cheese over the pork.
10. Fold the tortilla in half.
11. Grill for about 3 minutes, or until the tortilla is golden brown.
12. Carefully turn the quesadilla.
13. Grill for an additional 2 to 3 minutes, again, cook until the other side is golden brown.
14. Remove from heat, repeat with the other quesadillas.
15. Serve warm.

Pancetta Scallion Creamy Mac and Cheese

Serves: 4-6
Preparation time: 15 minutes
Cooking time: 40 minutes

Ingredients:

1 pound elbow macaroni, cooked
½ pound pancetta, cubed
2 cloves garlic, crushed and minced
½ cup scallions, sliced
¼ cup butter
¼ cup flour
3 cups milk or heavy cream
2 cups Swiss cheese, shredded
2 cups white cheddar cheese, shredded
½ cup parmesan cheese, freshly grated
1 teaspoon nutmeg
1 teaspoon paprika
2 teaspoons Dijon mustard
½ cup seasoned bread crumbs

Preparation:

1. Preheat oven to 400°F.
2. Prepare a 12-inch cast iron skillet and add the pancetta over medium-high heat. Cook until crispy, approximately 5 minutes. Add the garlic and scallions. Cook for 2 minutes. Remove with a slotted spoon and set aside.
3. Reduce heat to medium. Add the butter and cook until melted. Stir in the flour and mix until a thick, lightly browned paste is formed.
4. Slowly whisk in the milk or heavy cream. Bring to a boil while stirring constantly. Reduce heat to low and let simmer.

5. Add the Swiss cheese, cheddar cheese, parmesan, nutmeg, paprika and Dijon mustard. Stir well.
6. Add the cooked macaroni noodles and pancetta back into the pan. Mix well.
7. Top with seasoned bread crumbs, and additional parmesan cheese, if desired.
8. Place in the oven and bake for 30 minutes, or until browned.

Chorizo Tamale Pie

Serves: 4-6
Preparation time: 15 minutes
Cooking time: 30 minutes

Ingredients:
1 pound chorizo sausage, crumbled
1 cup red onion, diced
4 cloves garlic, crushed and minced
½ cup poblano pepper, diced
½ cup red bell pepper, diced
1 tablespoon ancho chili powder
2 teaspoons cumin
1 teaspoon coriander
¼ cup fresh cilantro, chopped
1 ½ cup fresh corn kernels
1 15 ounce can kidney beans, drained
1 28 ounce can tomatoes, crushed with liquid
1 cup vegetable or chicken stock
½ cup queso cheese, crumbled
½ cup cheddar cheese, shredded
½ cup butter, melted
1 cup cornmeal
1 cup flour
2 teaspoons baking powder
2 eggs, beaten
1 tablespoon orange juice
2 tablespoons honey
¼ cup buttermilk
1 cup sour cream
½ teaspoon salt

Preparation:

1. Preheat oven to 425°F.
2. Prepare a 12-inch cast iron skillet and add the chorizo over medium heat. Cook for 5 minutes.
3. Add the onion, garlic, poblano pepper, and red bell pepper. Cook, stirring frequently for 4-5 minutes. Season with ancho chili powder, cumin, coriander, and fresh cilantro. Stir well.
4. Add the corn kernels, kidney beans, tomatoes with liquid and vegetable or chicken stock. Increase heat to medium high and bring to a boil. Remove from heat and stir in the queso cheese and the cheddar cheese.
5. In a bowl, combine the cornmeal, flour, and baking powder. Slowly add the butter, eggs, orange juice, honey, buttermilk, sour cream, and salt. Mix until well blended.
6. Add the cornmeal mixture to the top of the skillet and spread evenly around.
7. Place the skillet in the oven and bake for 20 minutes, or until cornmeal crust is golden brown and firm.

Mushroom Pork Chops

Servings: 4
Preparation time: 10 minutes
Cooking time: 25 minutes

Ingredients:
4 pork chops, bone in (3/4" thickness)
1 teaspoon of fresh thyme
1 cup of wild mushrooms, sliced
1 teaspoon of salt
1 teaspoon of pepper
3/4 cup of beef broth
1 shallot
3 tablespoons of butter
2 teaspoons of Dijon mustard
1 /2 cup of red wine

Preparation:
1. Place a 12" cast iron skillet onto the stove, and set temperature to medium-high.
2. Wash and slice the mushrooms.
3. Place 1 1/2 tablespoons of butter into the skillet and melt.
4. Fold in the mushrooms, and cook until the mushrooms are golden brown, about 6 to 7 minutes.
5. Pour the mushrooms, along with the butter, into a bowl, set aside.
6. Return the cast iron skillet to the stove.
7. In a small bowl, whisk together the pepper and salt.
8. Rub the salt onto the pork chops.
9. Place the pork chops into the cast iron skillet, and cook until there is no pink left in the pork. This is usually 8 to 10 minutes on one side and then 8 to 10 minutes on the other.

10. Remove the pork from the skillet, and place in the oven to keep it warm.
11. Return the skillet to the stove.
12. Wash and chop the shallot. Add to the skillet.
13. Cook for about 2 minutes, making sure you scrape the bottom of the skillet as you cook.
14. Pour in the wine, and boil until the wine has been reduced by half, this usually takes about 2 minutes.
15. Fold in the beef broth.
16. Whisk in the mustard and remaining butter.
17. Fold in the thyme and cook for about 2 minutes or until it has thickened slightly.
18. Place the mushrooms back into the skillet, and cook until the mushrooms are hot, about 2 to 3 minutes.
19. Add the cooked pork chops to the mushroom sauce, and turn them to coat.
20. Serve warm with the mushroom sauce.

Cinnamon Scented Pork Medallions

Serves: 4
Preparation time: 10 minutes
Cooking time: 25 minutes

Ingredients:

1 pound pork tenderloin, cut into 1 inch thick medallions
½ teaspoon coarse sea salt
1 teaspoon cracked black pepper
1 tablespoon vegetable oil
3 cups asparagus spears, cut into 1 inch pieces
2 tablespoons butter
1 cinnamon stick
3 cups portabella or wild mushrooms, sliced
½ cup dry white wine
1 ½ cup chicken stock
½ teaspoon nutmeg
1 teaspoon thyme
1 tablespoon cornstarch
1 tablespoon cold water

Preparation:

1. Prepare a 12-inch deep cast iron skillet and heat the olive oil over medium high heat.
2. Season the pork medallions with salt and black pepper.
3. Add the pork to the pan and cook until browned, approximately 4-5 minutes per side.
4. Add the asparagus and sauté until color brightens, approximately 2-3 minutes.
5. Remove the pork medallions and asparagus to a serving plate.
6. Melt the butter over medium heat and add the cinnamon stick. Cook for 1-2 minutes or until fragrant.

7. Add the mushrooms and sauté for 2 minutes before adding the white wine. Reduce for 2-3 minutes.
8. Add the chicken stock, nutmeg and thyme. Let cook while you blend the cornstarch and water into a smooth paste.
9. Add the cornstarch mixture to the sauce. Cook while stirring until sauce thickens slightly.
10. Drizzle sauce over pork and asparagus before serving.

Easy Sweet Pea and Pork Casserole

Serves: 4
Preparation time: 10 minutes
Cooking time: 15 minutes

Ingredients:
1 pound ground pork
1 tablespoon olive oil
2 cloves garlic, crushed and minced
1 cup carrots, diced
½ cup celery, diced
2 cups fresh sweet peas
2 teaspoons fresh ginger, grated
2 teaspoons fresh lemongrass, chopped
2 tablespoons soy sauce
1 tablespoon oyster sauce
1 tablespoon rice vinegar
4 cups jasmine rice, cooked
1 teaspoon salt
1 teaspoon black pepper
Fresh scallions, chopped, for garnish

Preparation:
1. Prepare a 10- or 12-inch cast iron skillet and heat the oil over medium heat. Add the garlic, carrots, and celery. Cook while stirring, for 3-4 minutes.
2. Add the pork and cook until browned, approximately 5 minutes.
3. Add the peas and season with ginger, lemongrass, soy sauce, oyster sauce and rice vinegar. Mix well.
4. Add the rice and season with salt and black pepper. Heat through for an additional 3-4 minutes.
5. Serve garnished with fresh scallions.

Cherry-Glaze Pork Chops and Green Beans

Serves: 4
Preparation time: 10 minutes
Cooking time: 30 minutes

Ingredients:

4 pork chops
2 cups cherries, pitted, chopped
3 cloves garlic, minced
½ cup honey
1 lemon, juiced
1 cup low-sodium chicken stock
1 teaspoon paprika
Salt
Extra virgin olive oil

Preparation:

1. Generously sprinkle pork chops with salt, black pepper.
2. Heat 3 tablespoons extra virgin olive oil in medium cast iron skillet.
3. Brown pork chops over medium-high heat, 7-8 minutes. Remove from skillet.
4. In same skillet, add garlic, and sauté for 30 seconds.
5. Add green beans, sauté for another 3 minutes.
6. Add half cup of water, cover and cook for 5 minutes until tender.
7. Remove green beans to serving dish.
8. Add cherries, honey, lemon juice, chicken stock, 1 teaspoon salt to skillet, and bring to boil.
9. Return pork chops to skillet, reduce heat, simmer covered for 20 minutes.
10. Serve pork chops with green beans.

Italian Sausage Baked Spaghetti

Serves: 4
Preparation time: 10 minutes
Cooking time: 30 minutes

Ingredients:

1 pound ground Italian sausage
1 tablespoon vegetable oil
4 cloves garlic, crushed and minced
1 cup yellow onion, diced
1 28-ounce can crushed tomatoes, with liquid
¼ cup fresh parsley, chopped
½ cup fresh basil, chopped
1 tablespoon fresh oregano, chopped
1 teaspoon salt
1 teaspoon black pepper
2 cups chicken stock or water
½ pound spaghetti noodles
½ cup fresh mozzarella pearls
½ cup parmesan cheese, freshly grated

Preparation:

1. Preheat oven to 400°F
2. Prepare a 12-inch cast iron skillet and heat the vegetable oil over medium high heat. Add the Italian sausage to the pan and cook until browned, approximately 5-7 minutes. Drain any excess grease from the skillet.
3. Add the garlic and yellow onion. Sauté for 2-3 minutes, or until onions are tender.
4. Add the tomatoes, with liquid, and season with parsley, basil, oregano, salt, and black pepper. Stir well

5. Add the chicken stock or water and bring to a low boil. Add the pasta to the pan, pushing it in to make sure that the sauce covers the noodles. Cook for 10-12 minutes, or until pasta is al dente.
6. Mix in mozzarella and parmesan cheeses. Place skillet into the oven and bake for 15-20 minutes.

Lamb Kabobs with Shepherd's Salad

Serves: 4
Preparation time: 15 minutes
Cooking time: 10 minutes

Ingredients:
1 pound ground lamb
1 onion, minced
6 cloves garlic, minced
1 egg
2 tablespoons flour
½ teaspoon cinnamon
½ teaspoon cloves
1 teaspoon salt, black pepper

Shepherd's Salad
2 tomatoes, diced
1 English cucumber, diced
1 small onion, diced
2 lemons, juiced
2 tablespoons pomegranate syrup or honey
2 tablespoons vinegar
3 tablespoons extra virgin olive oil
1 teaspoon salt, black pepper

Preparation:
1. Whisk egg in bowl, mix in garlic, onion, flour, salt, and spices.
2. Gradually knead in ground lamb.
3. Shape 2" long cylindrical kabobs.
4. Heat ¼ cup olive oil in large cast iron skillet over medium heat, place kabobs in skillet.
5. Cook each side for approximately three minutes or until no longer pink inside.

6. In a bowl, whisk together vinegar, olive oil, salt, black pepper and lemon juice.
7. Place diced tomato, cucumber, and onion into dressing bowl and toss.
8. Serve kabobs with salad.

New York Sausage and Peppers Sandwich

Serves: 4
Preparation time: 10 minutes
Cooking time: 30 minutes

Ingredients:
4 Italian sausages
1 large onion, sliced
1 green bell pepper, seeded, sliced
1 red bell pepper, seeded sliced
1 cup tomato puree
½ teaspoon oregano
½ teaspoon cracked black pepper
Extra virgin olive oil

4 x 8" sesame submarine rolls

Preparation:
1. Heat 2 tablespoons extra virgin olive oil in cast iron deep skillet,
2. Add sausage, brown, and remove sausage from pan onto plate.
3. Add sliced bell peppers and onion to pan, and sauté for two minutes.
4. Return sausage to pan, cover with tomato puree.
5. Sprinkle dish with oregano, cracked black pepper, cover with a lid or foil and cook for 20 minutes.
6. Toast submarine rolls, and stuff with sausage and peppers.

Pork and Broccoli Skillet

Serves: 4
Preparation time: 10 minutes
Cooking time: 20 minutes

Ingredients:
1 pound pork loin roast
4 cups broccoli florets
4 cloves garlic, minced
1 medium onion, diced
¼ cup coconut aminos
½ teaspoon salt
1 teaspoon black pepper
1 cup low-sodium beef stock
Coconut oil

Preparation:
1. Slice pork loin roast into 1" pieces.
2. Heat 4 tablespoons coconut oil into cast iron skillet, add pork and sauté for two minutes.
3. Remove pork from skillet.
4. Into same pot, add garlic and onion, sauté for 30 seconds.
5. Add broccoli, continue to sauté for another minute.
6. Return pork to pot, add beef stock, coconut aminos, salt, black pepper, cover and cook on low for 15 mins.

BBQ Pork Chops

Serves: 6
Preparation time: 20 minutes
Cooking time: 45 minutes

Ingredients:
4 x 4 ounce boneless pork chops
2 cups tomato puree
3 dates, pitted
½ cup cashew, chopped
1 lemon, juiced
1 clove garlic, minced
1 teaspoon oregano
1 teaspoon salt
1 teaspoon black pepper
Extra light olive oil

Preparation:
1. Preheat oven to 400ºF.
2. Place dates in food processor and mix into paste. Add garlic, lemon juice, and tomato puree, mix, set aside.
3. Heat 4 tablespoons extra virgin olive oil in cast iron skillet over medium-high heat.
4. Sear pork chops, top with BBQ sauce from blender, slide into oven, and cook for 35 minutes, turning halfway through.
5. Serve with Garlic Asparagus Sauté (recipe in Vegetarian).

Pork Loin with Sweet Potato

Serves: 2
Preparation time: 15 minutes
Cooking time: 55 minutes

Ingredients:

1 pound pork loin roast
1 sweet potato, peeled, sliced
1 red apple, cored, sliced
1 celery stalk, chopped
1 clove garlic, minced
1 teaspoon salt
1 teaspoon black pepper
Extra virgin olive oil

Preparation:

1. Preheat oven to 400ºF.
2. Heat 4 tablespoons extra virgin olive oil in skillet, place pork loin in skillet and brown.
3. Remove pork loin to plate.
4. Place sweet potato, apples, onions, celery, garlic on bottom of cast iron skillet, top with pork loin roast, and slide into oven for 45 minutes.

Lamb and Butternut Squash Stew

Serves: 4
Preparation time: 15 minutes
Cooking time: 50 minutes

Ingredients:
1 butternut squash
12 ounces lamb
1 medium onion, sliced
3 cups water
3 tablespoons ghee
½ lemon, juiced
Salt and black pepper

Garnish
Parsley

Preparation:
1. Peel butternut squash, chop into 1" cubes, place aside.
2. Cut lamb into 1" cubes.
3. Heat ghee in cast iron pot, add lamb and brown.
4. Add onion, sauté.
5. Add butternut squash, lemon juice, water and salt, black pepper to taste.
6. Cover cast iron pot, and cook for 45 minutes or until squash is tender.

Middle Eastern Spiced Lamb

Serve: 6
Preparation time: 5 minutes
Cooking time: 50 minutes

Ingredients:

2 pounds boneless lamb loin
¼ cup dried apricots
¼ cup walnuts
¼ cup plum
3 teaspoons ginger, grated
1 teaspoon cinnamon
1 teaspoon salt
1 teaspoon black pepper
Coconut oil

Preparation:

1. Preheat oven to 400ºF.
2. Slice boneless lamb chops into1" cubes and sprinkle with 1 teaspoon salt.
3. Heat 4 tablespoons coconut oil in cast iron skillet over medium heat.
4. Brown lamb.
5. Reduce heat to medium low, add apricots, walnuts, plum ginger cinnamon, salt, black pepper.
6. Place into oven for 45 minutes.
7. Serve with Flax Tortilla (recipe in Sides and Accompaniments) for scooping.

Fish and Seafood

Shrimp Piccata

Serves: 4
Preparation time: 10 minutes
Cooking time: 15 minutes

Ingredients:
1 pound raw shrimp, cleaned and deveined
2 tablespoons butter
3 cloves garlic, crushed and minced
¼ cup shallots, sliced
¼ cup capers
¼ cup lemon juice
1 cup dry white wine
1 ½ cups chicken stock
1 teaspoon salt
1 teaspoon black pepper
½ pound angel hair pasta
Fresh parsley for garnish

Preparation:
1. Prepare a 10- or 12-inch cast iron skillet and melt the butter over medium heat.
2. Add the garlic and shallots. Cook for 1-2 minutes.
3. Add the shrimp, gently tossing while cooking, for 2 minutes.
4. Add the capers, lemon juice, and white wine to the skillet. Let the wine reduce for 1-2 minutes.
5. Add the chicken stock, salt, and black pepper. Stir well. Increase heat to medium high and bring to a low boil.
6. Add the angel hair pasta, reduce heat back down to medium and cook for 7-10 minutes, or until pasta is al dente.
7. Serve garnished with fresh parsley.

Shrimp and Chorizo Paella

Serves: 4-6
Preparation time: 10 minutes
Cooking time: 40 minutes

Ingredients:
¼ cup olive oil
1 cup red onion, diced
1 cup green bell pepper, diced
4 cloves garlic, crushed and minced
1 pound chorizo sausage, crumbled
¼ cup tomato paste
1 teaspoon smoked paprika
½ teaspoon cayenne powder
1 cup dry white wine
1 cup chicken stock
3 cups cooked rice
½ pound raw shrimp, cleaned and deveined.

Preparation:
1. Preheat the oven to 425°F.
2. Prepare a 10- or 12-inch cast iron skillet and heat the olive oil over medium heat.
3. Add the chorizo and cook until browned, approximately 5 minutes. Drain off any excess grease.
4. Add the red onion, green bell pepper and garlic. Sauté until onions and pepper just begin to become tender, approximately 4 minutes.
5. Season with tomato paste, smoked paprika, and cayenne powder. Stir well.
6. Add the white wine and let reduce 5 minutes. Add the chicken stock and cooked rice. Stir well.
7. Place the skillet in the oven and bake for 20 minutes. Remove and add the shrimp.
8. Place the skillet back in the oven and bake for an additional 10 minutes or until shrimp are cooked through.

White Wine Braised Salmon and Baked Potatoes

Serves: 4
Preparation time: 10 minutes
Cooking time: 25 minutes

Ingredients:

1 pound salmon fillets
1 tablespoon olive oil
2 cloves garlic, crushed and minced
1 tablespoon fresh dill
1 tablespoon fresh chives
1 teaspoon lemon zest
½ cup dry white wine
3 cups green beans, washed and trimmed
4 cups yellow potatoes, sliced thin
2 teaspoons fresh rosemary
1 teaspoon salt
1 teaspoon black pepper

Preparation:

1. Preheat oven to 425°F.
2. Prepare a 10-inch cast iron skillet and heat the olive oil over medium heat. Add the garlic and sauté 1 minute.
3. Add the salmon and season with dill, chives, and lemon zest. Add the white wine to the skillet and cook for two minutes.
4. Add the green beans to the pan. Then layer the potato slices evenly over the salmon and green beans. Season the potatoes with rosemary, salt, and black pepper.
5. Place the skillet in the oven and bake for 15-20 minutes, or until salmon is flaky and pink.

Cajun Shrimp Alfredo

Serves: 4
Preparation time: 10 minutes
Cooking time: 20 minutes

Ingredients:
½ cup butter
¼ cup shallots, sliced
3 cloves garlic, crushed and minced
¼ cup dry white wine
¼ cup flour
1 cup chicken stock
2 cups heavy cream
2 teaspoons Cajun seasoning
1 teaspoon salt
1 teaspoon black pepper
1 cup parmesan cheese, freshly grated
1 pound shrimp, cleaned and deveined
½ pound linguine noodles
Lemon wedges for garnish

Preparation:
1. Prepare a 12-inch cast iron skillet and melt butter over medium heat.
2. Add the garlic and the shallots. Sauté for 1-2 minutes.
3. Add the white wine and let reduce for 2 minutes before stirring in the flour. Mix using a spoon until the flour has blended into a smooth paste.
4. Slowly add the chicken stock and heavy cream, stirring constantly. Season with Cajun seasoning, salt, and black pepper. Stir in the parmesan cheese.
5. Cook the pasta over medium heat for 7-10 minutes, or until al dente.
6. Add the shrimp to the sauce and simmer for 2-3 minutes before adding the pasta.
7. Serve with fresh lemon as garnish.

Pecan Fried Catfish

Servings: 6
Preparation time: 1 hour and 10 minutes
Cooking time: 10 minutes

Ingredients:
2 pounds of catfish fillets (3 to 4 fillets depending on size)
1 tablespoon of Cajun seasoning
2/3 cup of Parmesan cheese
1 cup of buttermilk
1 tablespoon of paprika
1 cup of ground pecans
2 eggs
2/3 cup of cornmeal
2 cups of vegetable oil

Preparation:
1. Cut the catfish into 1" wide strips.
2. Place the catfish into a large freezer bag.
3. Pour in the buttermilk.
4. Close the bag and shake. Place in the fridge, and allow the catfish to marinate for about an hour.
5. While the catfish is marinating, whisk together the ground pecans and cornmeal.
6. Fold in the Cajun seasoning and the paprika.
7. Remove the catfish from the fridge, and remove from the buttermilk. Discard the buttermilk.
8. Whisk the eggs together in a separate bowl.
9. Dip the catfish into the eggs so that they are completely coated.
10. Toss them in the cornmeal mixture, and coat completely.
11. Place on a baking sheet until you are ready to cook the fish.

12. In a large, 12" cast iron skillet, pour in enough oil to fill the skillet about 1 1/2 inches deep.
13. Place on the stove, and set heat to medium-high.
14. Bring the oil to a slow boil.
15. Place the catfish into the cast iron skillet, and fry until it is golden brown, turning as needed. This usually takes between 3 to 6 minutes. You also want to make sure the fish flakes with a fork. You may need to cook in batches.
16. Remove from oil and allow to drain.
17. Serve warm.

Oyster Brunch

Servings: 6
Preparation time: 15 minutes
Cooking time: 45 minutes

Ingredients:
1/4 pound of Tasso
2 cups of canned oysters, drained (1 -15ounce can)
1/4 pound of bacon (6 to 10 slices)
1 cup of yellow onion, chopped
2 garlic cloves, minced
1 cup of sliced mushrooms
2 tablespoons of fresh parsley leaves
1/2 cup of white cheddar cheese, shredded
1/2 cup of green bell peppers, chopped
1 teaspoon of fresh tarragon leaves, chopped
1 teaspoon of salt
1/4 teaspoon of cayenne pepper, ground
1 cup of regular grits
1/4 cup of heavy cream
4 cups of milk

Preparation:
1. Place a 12" cast iron skillet onto the stove and set the temperature to medium high.
2. Chop up the bacon, and add it to the skillet.
3. Cook for about 2 minutes.
4. Chop the Tasso, and add it to the bacon. Cook until the bacon is crisp, usually about 3 to 5 minutes.
5. Remove the bacon and Tasso with a slotted spoon, and place on a paper towel to drain.
6. Remove 2 tablespoons of the fat from the skillet, and then drain the rest.
7. Return the reserved fat.

8. Wash, peel, and chop the onions. Place in the skillet.
9. Wash, seed, and chop the bell peppers, add to the onions.
10. Cook the vegetables until they are tender, about 3 to 5 minutes.
11. Mince the garlic, and add to the onions. Cook until you can smell the garlic, about 30 seconds.
12. Wash and slice the mushrooms, add to the onion mixture.
13. Fold in the cayenne pepper and salt.
14. Wash and chop the parsley and tarragon. Add to the onion mixture.
15. Continue to cook until the mushrooms are soft, about 3 to 5 minutes.
16. Drain the oyster liquid and reserve about 1/2 a cup.
17. Whisk that into a bowl with the milk.
18. Pour over the mushroom mixture and bring to a boil.
19. Add the grits, stirring constantly until it is boiling again.
20. Once it is boiling, reduce the heat to low, and cover the skillet with a lid.
21. Simmer for 20 to 30 minutes, or until the grits have absorbed most of the liquid.
22. Add the oysters and the bacon mixture. Stir well.
23. Fold in the cream.
24. Increase the heat to medium, and continue to cook until the oysters begin to curl on the edges. This usually takes about 5 minutes.
25. Shred the cheese.
26. Remove the skillet from the stove.
27. Sprinkle the cheese over the entire dish.
28. Serve warm.

Dill Butter Salmon and Rice

Serves: 4
Preparation time: 10 minutes
Cooking time: 25 minutes

Ingredients:
4 salmon fillets
2 tablespoons fresh dill, chopped
4 tablespoons butter
2 teaspoons chives, chopped
1 teaspoon salt
Extra virgin olive oil

Lemon Rice
1 cup rice
2 lemons, juiced
½ teaspoon cumin seeds
1 teaspoon salt
Extra virgin olive oil

Preparation:
1. Preheat oven to 350 degrees.
2. Heat 3 Tablespoons olive oil in large cast iron skillet over medium.
3. Add salmon, cook for a minute, and turn over.
4. Add butter, sprinkle with dill, salt, and chives, and cook for 2 minutes.
5. Place skillet in oven, and bake for 10 minutes.
6. Wash rice, bring large pot of water to boil.
7. Cook rice in water for 10 minutes, drain.
8. In small cast iron pan, heat 3 tablespoons extra virgin olive oil, add cumin seeds, sauté for a minute, add lemon juice, salt, black pepper, remove from heat, and drizzle over rice.
9. Serve rice with Dill Butter Salmon.

Pineapple Shrimp Stir Fry

Serves: 4
Preparation time: 10 minutes
Cooking time: 10 minutes

Ingredients:
1 pound shrimp, peeled and deveined
½ cup chopped pineapple
½ cup shallots, chopped
1 lemon, juiced
1 teaspoon salt
Extra virgin olive oil

Preparation:
1. Heat 3 tablespoons olive oil in medium cast iron skillet, add shallots, sauté for 2 minutes.
2. Add pineapple, sauté for 3-4 minutes or until a caramelization begins to take place.
3. Sprinkle in salt, add shrimp, sauté until pink, remove from heat.
4. Allow shrimp to sit in pineapple for a few minutes to soak in juices before serving.
5. Squeeze lemon juice over shrimp and serve with rice or noodles.

Shrimp Jambalaya

Servings: 6
Preparation time: 30 minutes
Cooking time: 45 minutes

Ingredients:
1 pound of sausage
1 pound of ham, smoked and cubed
1 pound of shrimp, deveined (about 20 to 24 shrimp)
6 cups of chicken stock
1 tablespoon of olive oil
1 red bell pepper
1 green bell pepper
1 jalapeno pepper
1/2 cup of scallions, diced
1 onion
3 garlic cloves
1 cup of celery, diced
3/4 cup of fresh parsley, chopped
1 cup of tomatoes, seeded and diced
3 bay leaves
1/4 cup of lemon juice
1 tablespoon of butter
2 tablespoons of tomato paste
2 teaspoons of salt
1 teaspoon of black pepper
2 teaspoons of oregano, dried
1 teaspoon of thyme, dried
3 cups of long grain rice

Preparation:

1. In a large, 12" cast iron skillet, heat the oil over medium heat on the stove.
2. Slice the sausage, and place it in the oil.
3. Cube the ham, and place in the skillet with the sausage.
4. Sauté the meat until it is browned, about 8 to 10 minutes.
5. Remove the meat, and set aside.
6. Return the cast iron skillet to the stove.
7. Add the butter, and allow it to melt.
8. Wash and chop the celery.
9. Wash, peel, and dice the onion. Add the celery and onion to the skillet.
10. Wash, seed, and chop the red and green bell peppers. Add to the skillet.
11. Cook the vegetables until the onion is tender, about 8 to 10 minutes.
12. Wash, seed, and dice the tomatoes and jalapeno pepper.
13. Add to the pan, along with the tomato paste, oregano and thyme.
14. Mince the garlic, and stir into the mixture.
15. Cook until all the vegetables are beginning to become tender, about 5 minutes.
16. Pour in the chicken stock, and bring the ingredients to a boil.
17. Rinse the rice, and place into the skillet.
18. Fold in the sausage mixture. Mix until the ingredients are fully incorporated.
19. Season with salt and pepper, and add the bay leaves.
20. Bring to a boil before reducing the heat to low.
21. Cover and simmer for about 20 minutes.
22. When the time is done, add the shrimp to the mixture.
23. Wash and chop the scallions and parsley. Add to the rice mixture, along with the lemon juice.
24. Mix the ingredients until they are well blended.
25. Cover the skillet again, and remove from heat. Let sit for 15 minutes.
26. Serve warm.

Smokey Bacon and Crab Chowder

Serves: 4-6
Preparation time: 10 minutes
Cooking time: 30 minutes

Ingredients:
½ pound bacon, diced
1 cup sweet yellow onion, diced
1 cup celery, diced
1 cup carrots, diced
1 tablespoon fresh thyme
1 teaspoon salt
1 teaspoon black pepper
½ cup dry white wine
8 cups red potatoes, cubed
2 cups whole milk
2 cups fish stock
1 cup heavy cream
1 cup clam juice
1 pound crab meat
Fresh scallions for garnish

Preparation:
1. Prepare a 12-inch skillet and cook the bacon over medium heat until lightly crisp, approximately 5 minutes.
2. Add yellow onion, celery, and carrots. Season with thyme, salt, and black pepper. Sauté for 3-4 minutes. Add the white wine and cook 1-2 minutes more.
3. Add the potatoes, milk, fish stock, heavy cream, and crab juice. Stir well. Increase heat to medium high and cook, stirring frequently until potatoes are tender, approximately 10 minutes.

4. Transfer half of the mixture to a blender and blend until smooth. Reincorporate the blended mixture back into the skillet.
5. Add the crab meat and cook until heated through, approximately 7-10 minutes.
6. Garnish with fresh scallions.

Sweet and Spicy Scallops

Serves: 4
Preparation time: 10 minutes
Cooking time: 15 minutes

Ingredients:
2 teaspoons olive oil
6 cups bok choy, cut into chunks
2 tablespoons butter
16-20 sea scallops
4 cloves garlic crushed and minced
1 tablespoon jalapeno pepper, diced
½ cup sugar
¼ cup rice vinegar
½ cup water
1 teaspoon salt
1 teaspoon black pepper

Preparation:
1. Prepare a 10 or 12-inch cast iron skillet and heat the olive oil over medium heat. Add the bok choy and sauté until crisp tender, approximately 4-5 minutes. Remove from the pan and set aside. Keep warm.
2. Add the butter to the skillet and melt over medium heat. Add the scallops, garlic and jalapeno pepper. Cook the scallops 1-2 minutes per side, while lightly tossing the other ingredients.
3. Add the sugar, rice vinegar, and water to the skillet. Stir well and let cook for 3-4 minutes, allowing flavors to blend.
4. Serve scallops and sauce over sautéed bok choy.

Spicy Lemon Whitefish

Serves: 4
Preparation time: 10 minutes
Cooking time: 15 minutes

Ingredients:
1 pound whitefish fillets
¼ cup butter
1 teaspoon smoked paprika
½ teaspoon cayenne powder
2 teaspoons crushed red pepper flakes
2 cloves garlic, crushed and minced
1 teaspoon salt
1 teaspoon black pepper
1 cup vegetable or chicken stock
2 tablespoons lemon juice
4 cups dark leafy greens, such as chard
2 teaspoons lemon zest
Fresh lemon wedges for garnish
Cayenne pepper sauce for serving

Preparation:
1. In a bowl, combine the paprika, cayenne powder, crushed red pepper, garlic, salt, and black pepper. Season both sides of the whitefish fillets with the spice mixture.
2. Prepare a 12-inch cast iron skillet and melt the butter over medium heat. Add the fish to the pan and cook for approximately 3 minutes on each side.
3. Add the vegetable or chicken stock and lemon juice to the pan. Add the dark, leafy greens and lemon zest. Toss lightly. Continue cooking over medium heat for 4-5 minutes or until greens are tender.
4. Garnish with fresh lemons and serve with cayenne pepper sauce for extra spice on the greens.

Orange Cranberry Tilapia Salad

Serves: 2
Preparation time: 10 minutes
Cooking time: 10 minutes

Ingredients:
2 Tilapia filets
2 mandarin oranges, segmented
¼ cup sunflower seeds
¼ cup dried cranberry
2 cups leafy lettuce, chopped
1 tablespoon lemon juice
1 teaspoon salt, black pepper
Extra virgin olive oil

Preparation:
1. Heat 3 tablespoons olive oil in large cast iron skillet over medium heat.
2. Add Tilapia filets and cook 3 minutes per side, set aside.
3. In bowl, toss orange segments, cranberry, lettuce, sunflower seeds, drizzle with 3 tablespoons olive oil and lemon juice.
4. Serve Tilapia atop salad.

Wild Salmon with Yellow Squash

Serves: 4
Preparation time: 15 minutes
Cooking time: 15 minutes

Ingredients:
4 x 4 ounce wild salmon fillets (1" thick)
2 medium yellow squash, sliced
2 fennel bulbs, sliced into strips
¼ cup sliced almonds
1 lemon, juiced
1 teaspoon lemon peel, grated
¼ cup ghee
Salt and black pepper
Almond oil

Preparation:
1. Heat almond oil in your cast iron skillet over medium heat.
2. Add squash, fennel, and almonds, and sauté until veggies are tender. Remove to dish and toss with lemon juice, salt, and black pepper.
3. Add ghee into same cast iron skillet, and heat on medium.
4. Place salmon fillets skin-side up in heated skillet. Cook for 5 minutes, gently turn over, and cook for 4 minutes.
5. Serve salmon with veggies.

Prosciutto-Wrapped Cod Filet and Zucchini

Serves: 4
Preparation time: 10 minutes
Cooking time: 20 minutes

Ingredients:
4 x 4 ounce cod filets
4 slices prosciutto ham
2 cups chicken stock
¼ cup sundried tomato, chopped
2 cloves garlic, grated
Salt and black pepper
Coconut oil

Preparation:
1. Preheat oven to 400°F.
2. In bowl combine garlic, ½ teaspoon salt, ½ teaspoon black pepper and mix.
3. Wrap each cod fillet with a prosciutto slice.
4. Heat 4 tablespoons coconut oil in cast iron skillet, add cod filets to skillet and cook 3 minutes per side.
5. Add sundried tomato and garlic mixture to skillet, and place into the oven for 15 minutes.
6. Plate prosciutto-wrapped cod fillet with ZuCa Noodles (recipe in Vegetarian and Side category).

Fish Tacos with Orange Cilantro Salad

Serves: 4
Preparation time: 10 minutes
Cooking time: 10 minutes

Ingredients
16 ounces Tilapia filets
1 teaspoon fresh ginger, grated
½ red bell pepper, seeded, diced
1 green onion, chopped
1 green chili pepper, seeded, minced
8 leaves Boston lettuce
2 cups cilantro, chopped
1/3 cup natural orange juice
1 tablespoon coconut aminos
Extra virgin olive oil
Salt and black pepper

Preparation:
1. For the filling, heat 4 tablespoons of extra virgin olive oil in cast iron skillet on medium heat. Place Tilapia filets in cast iron skillet, and cook for 4 minutes per side.
2. Remove fish to plate, and using fork, separate fish into small pieces. Mix with ginger, coconut aminos, red bell pepper, and a ½ teaspoon each of salt and black pepper.
3. Combine green onions, chili pepper, and cilantro in a bowl, drizzle with orange juice, add salt and black pepper to taste and toss.
4. Stack two leaves Boston lettuce on flat surface, spoon in some of the Tilapia filling, top with orange cilantro salad, wrap, and enjoy.

Note: You can also wrap your fish tacos in flaxseed tortillas (recipe in Vegetarian and Side category).

Garlic Shrimp in Mushroom Vestibules

Serve: 4
Preparation time: 15 minutes
Cooking time: 35 minutes

Ingredients:
½ pound shrimp
½ red bell pepper, seeded, finely-chopped
1 celery stalk, finely chopped
4 Portabella mushrooms
1 cup coconut milk
¼ cup ghee, melted
1 lemon, juiced
½ teaspoon rosemary
1 teaspoon salt
1 teaspoon black pepper
Extra virgin olive oil

Preparation:
1. Preheat oven to 400ºF.
2. Heat ghee in cast iron skillet, add garlic, bell pepper, and celery stalk, and sauté for two minutes.
3. Add shrimp, salt, black pepper, and rosemary, and sauté until shrimp is pink. Remove shrimp and veggies to plate.
4. In the same skillet, place portabella mushrooms upside down in skillet.
5. Spoon equal amount shrimp in each Portabella mushrooms, pour coconut milk over each Portabella mushroom, allowing it to leak into skillet.
6. Place into oven, and bake for 25 minutes.

Shrimp and Sausage Gumbo

Serves: 6
Preparation time: 10 minutes
Cooking time: 25 minutes

Ingredients:
1 pound Andouille sausages
1 pound shrimp
1 red bell pepper, seeded, diced
1 green bell pepper, seeded, diced
1 carrot, peeled, diced
1 celery stalk, diced
1 red onion, sliced
1 cup cauliflower florets, grated
2 cups tomatoes, diced
2 cups low-sodium chicken stock
1 teaspoon black pepper
1 teaspoon salt
1 bay leaf
Extra virgin olive oil

Preparation:
1. Slice Andouille sausage into ½" thick slices.
2. Heat 3 tablespoons extra virgin olive oil in cast iron skillet over medium heat.
3. Add onion and garlic, and sauté.
4. Add bell peppers, celery stalk, and carrot, and sauté for 3 minutes.
5. Add tomatoes, chicken stock, black pepper, salt, bay leaf, and cauliflower.
6. Cover skillet, and cook for 20 minutes over medium heat.
7. Add shrimp, cook for a minute, and remove from heat.
8. Serve hot.

Vegetarian and Side

Root Vegetable Pot Pie

Serves: 4-6
Preparation time: 15 minutes
Cooking time: 50 minutes

Ingredients:

2 tablespoon olive oil
1 cup yellow onion, sliced
3 cloves garlic, crushed and minced
1 cups red potatoes, cubed
1 cup carrots, sliced
1 cup sweet potato, cubed
1 cup beets, cubed
½ cup butter
¼ cup + 1 tablespoon flour
1 ½ cup vegetable stock
1 cup heavy cream
1 teaspoon tarragon
½ teaspoon celery seed
1 teaspoon oregano
1 teaspoon salt
1 teaspoon black pepper
2 refrigerated pie crusts doughs

Preparation:

1. Preheat oven to 425°F.
2. Take one of the pie crust doughs and lay it flat. Using a small cookie cutter, approximately 1-2 inches in any shape, cut out as many pieces as possible from the dough and set aside. These will be used to for decorative edging that will bridge the crust gap in the skillet.

3. Prepare a 10-inch skillet and heat the olive oil over medium. Add the onions and garlic. Sauté until tender, approximately 2-3 minutes.
4. Add the red potatoes, carrots, sweet potatoes, and beets. Cook while stirring occasionally until the vegetables just begin to tenderize, approximately 7 minutes. Remove from the pan and set aside.
5. Add the butter to the pan and cook until melted. Add the flour and stir constantly until a browned paste is formed. Slowly add the vegetable stock and heavy cream, whisking constantly to smoothly incorporate the flour mixture until a thick sauce is formed.
6. Season with tarragon, celery seed, oregano, salt, and black pepper. Add the vegetables back in and stir. Remove pan from the heat and let cool slightly.
7. Place one pie crust over the center of the pan. Use the pieces that were cut out to bridge the space between the crust and the rim of the pan all around the edge. Press gently to seal.
8. Place in the oven and bake for 30-35 minutes, or until crust is golden brown.

Creamy Green Vegetable Skillet Pasta

Serves: 4
Preparation time: 10 minutes
Cooking time: 15 minutes

Ingredients:
¼ cup butter
2 cloves garlic, crushed and minced
¼ cup scallions, sliced
2 cups broccoli florets
2 cups zucchini, sliced
2 cups spinach, torn
½ teaspoon crushed red pepper flakes
1 teaspoon salt
1 teaspoon black pepper
1 cup vegetable stock
½ cup heavy cream
½ cup cream cheese, softened
½ cup parmesan cheese, freshly grated
¼ cup fresh basil, chopped
½ cup fresh parsley, chopped
1 tablespoon fresh chives, chopped
1 pound bow tie pasta, cooked
Lemon zest for garnish, if desired

Preparation:
1. Prepare a 12-inch cast iron skillet and heat the butter over medium heat. Add the garlic and scallions, cook for 1 minute.
2. Add the broccoli and zucchini. Sauté for 2-3 minutes. Add the spinach to the skillet and sauté for 1-2 additional minutes. Season with crushed red pepper, salt, and black pepper.

3. Remove the vegetable mixture from the skillet and set aside.
4. To the skillet, add the vegetable stock over medium high heat and bring almost to a boil. Reduce heat to medium. Slowly stir in the heavy cream and add the cream cheese, stirring the entire time, until a smooth consistency is achieved.
5. Reduce heat to low and add the parmesan cheese, basil, parsley, and chives. Mix well.
6. Add the vegetables and pasta back to the pan and toss well to mix. Let simmer for 3-4 minutes, or until warmed through.
7. Serve garnished with lemon zest, if desired.

Buttermilk Cornbread

Servings: 6
Preparation time: 10 minutes
Cooking time: 30 minutes

Ingredients:
2 cups of buttermilk
1 cup of cornmeal
1 teaspoon of baking powder
1/2 teaspoon of baking soda
1 cup of flour, all purpose
2 tablespoons of sugar
2 eggs
3 tablespoons of butter

Preparation:
1. Preheat the oven to 375°F.
2. Add the butter to a 10" cast iron skillet.
3. Place in the oven while you make the batter.
4. In a large bowl, whisk together the flour, baking soda, and baking powder.
5. Add the cornmeal, and mix until the ingredients are well blended.
6. In a separate bowl, cream together the eggs and buttermilk.
7. Add the sugar, and blend until the sugar is dissolved.
8. Remove the cast iron skillet from the oven, and tilt the skillet until it is completely coated in butter.
9. Pour the remaining butter into the egg mixture.
10. Add the wet ingredients into the dry, and mix until the batter is smooth.
11. Pour the batter into the cast iron skillet, and place in the oven.
12. Bake for 25 to 30 minutes or until the cornbread golden brown and springs back when pressed.
13. Serve warm on its own or with another dish.

Ooey-Gooey Mac'n Cheese

Serves: 6
Preparation time: 10 minutes
Cooking time: 15 minutes

Ingredients:
2 cups elbow macaroni
1 cup aged Cheddar, grated
1 cup Emmental cheese, grated
½ cup Romano, grated
¼ cup butter
½ cup flour
3 cups milk (full fat)
½ teaspoon dry mustard
1 teaspoon salt, white pepper

Preparation:
1. Preheat broiler.
2. Bring a large pot of water to boil, add a teaspoon of salt to boiling water, and mix in elbow macaroni.
3. Cook macaroni according to package direction, drain, set aside.
4. Place a cast iron deep skillet or a Dutch oven on the stove, over medium heat, add butter, and melt.
5. In a bowl, mix in flour until paste begins to form, and whisk in milk until a thinner version of the paste forms.
6. Add half of the cheddar, and all of remaining cheeses, salt, white pepper, and mustard, and mix until saucy.
7. Add pasta to cast iron, mix well, sprinkle with remaining cheddar cheese, and broil in oven for 5 minutes.
8. Serve hot.

Bok Choy Chinese Noodles

Serves: 4
Preparation time: 10 minutes
Cooking time: 15 minutes

Ingredients:
¼ cup peanut oil
1 pound baby bok choy, halved lengthwise
1 cup vegetable stock
¼ cup creamy natural peanut butter
2 tablespoons soy sauce
2 teaspoons chili garlic paste
1 teaspoon honey
1 tablespoon fresh grated ginger
2 cloves garlic, crushed and minced
½ teaspoon crushed red pepper flakes
12 ounces Chinese flat noodles, cooked
2 teaspoons sesame oil
Scallions, sliced for garnish

Preparation:
1. Prepare a 10-inch cast iron skillet and add the peanut oil over medium heat. Add the bok choy and cook for 2 minutes on each side. Remove from pan and set aside.
2. To the skillet, add the vegetable stock, peanut butter, and soy sauce. Stir while cooking over medium heat until smooth.
3. Add the chili garlic paste, honey, fresh ginger, garlic, and crushed red pepper. Mix well.
4. Add the noodles to the skillet and toss.
5. Arrange the bok choy on serving plates. Place equal portions of the noodles over the box choy and drizzle with sesame oil.
6. Garnish with scallions before serving.

Lemony Wild Mushroom and Broccoli Pasta

Serves: 4
Preparation time: 10 minutes
Cooking time: 15 minutes

Ingredients:
2 cups broccoli florets
2 tablespoons olive oil, divided
2 cloves garlic, crushed and minced
3 cups vegetable stock or water
1 pound linguine noodles
4 cups wild mushrooms, thinly sliced
2 tablespoons lemon juice
1 tablespoon lemon zest
2 teaspoons fresh thyme
1 tablespoon fresh chives
1 teaspoon salt
1 teaspoon black pepper
Fresh grated asiago cheese for garnish

Preparation:
1. In a bowl combine the wild mushrooms, 1 tablespoon of olive oil, lemon juice, lemon zest, thyme, chives, salt, and black pepper. Toss to mix.
2. Prepare a 10- or 12-inch cast iron skillet and heat 1 tablespoon of olive oil over medium heat. Add the broccoli florets and sauté until bright green and slightly tender. Transfer to the bowl with the mushrooms and set aside.
3. Add the vegetable stock or water to the skillet and heat over medium high until lightly boiling. Add the linguine noodles and cook for approximately 7-10 minutes, or until al dente. Drain excess liquid.
4. Transfer the broccoli and mushroom mixture to the pan with the linguine. Toss, while heating over medium low heat until all ingredients are warmed through and nicely blended.
5. Toss with fresh asiago cheese before serving.

178

Zesty Eggplant Parmesan

Serves: 4
Preparation time: 10 minutes
Cooking time: 30 minutes

Ingredients:
¼ cup vegetable oil
1 medium-sized eggplant, sliced approximately ¼ inch thick
2 eggs, beaten
1 cup seasoned bread crumbs
1 clove garlic, crushed and minced
1 cup parmesan cheese, freshly grated, divided
2 ½ cups prepared marinara sauce (homemade or jarred)
1 tablespoon fresh oregano
¼ cup fresh basil, chopped (additional for garnish, if desired)
1 teaspoon salt
1 teaspoon black pepper
1 cup fresh mozzarella cheese, sliced
6 cups dark salad greens, for serving.

Preparation:
1. Preheat oven to 350°F.
2. Place the beaten eggs in one bowl, and in another bowl combine the seasoned bread crumbs, garlic and ½ cup parmesan cheese.
3. Prepare a 12-inch cast iron skillet and heat the vegetable oil over medium high heat.
4. Coat each eggplant slice with the beaten egg and then dredge through the breadcrumb mixture.
5. Place the eggplant slices in the pan and cook 2 minutes per side, or until browned. Reserve cooked pieces of eggplant on a side plate as you work through the eggplant in batches.

6. Turn off the heat and layer all pieces of eggplant in the bottom of the skillet. Top with marinara sauce and season with oregano, basil, salt, and black pepper.
7. Top the eggplant with mozzarella cheese and remaining ½ cup parmesan cheese.
8. Place in the oven and bake for 20 minutes or until cheese is golden brown.
9. Serve with fresh dark salad greens.

Sweet Potato Burrito Skillet

Serves: 4
Preparation time: 10 minutes
Cooking time: 30 minutes

Ingredients:
2 ½ cups sweet potatoes, cubed
¼ cup olive oil, divided
1 cup yellow onion, diced
3 cloves garlic, crushed and minced
1 cup red bell peppers, chopped
2 cups tomatoes, diced
1 cup rice
1 15-ounce can black beans, drained
1 ½ cup fresh corn kernels
1 teaspoon chili powder
1 teaspoon cumin
1 teaspoon paprika
1 teaspoon salt
1 teaspoon black pepper
¼ cup fresh cilantro, chopped
2 ½ cups vegetable broth
1 cup Mexican queso cheese
1 cup cheddar cheese
Sour cream for garnish

Preparation:

1. Prepare a 10- or 12-inch cast iron skillet and heat 2 tablespoons of olive oil over medium heat. Add the sweet potatoes and cook, while stirring, for approximately 7-8 minutes.
2. Add the onion, garlic, and red bell pepper, along with an additional 2 tablespoons of olive oil, if needed. Cook for 5 minutes more.
3. Add the tomatoes, rice, black beans, and corn kernels. Toss to mix and season with chili powder, cumin, paprika, salt, black pepper, and cilantro.
4. Add the vegetable broth and increase heat until broth boils. Reduce heat and allow to simmer for 15 minutes, or until rice is tender.
5. Stir in queso and Mexican cheeses and let melt before serving.
6. Garnish with sour cream.

White Bean and Southern Greens Chili

Serves: 4-6
Preparation time: 10 minutes
Cooking time: 30 minutes

Ingredients:
1 tablespoon olive oil
1 cup yellow onion, diced
3 cloves garlic, crushed and minced
1 cup green bell pepper, diced
1 cup tomatillos, chopped
2 cups collard greens, chopped
1 teaspoon cumin
1 tablespoon chili powder
1 tablespoon lime juice
¼ cup fresh cilantro, chopped
3 cups cannellini beans, cooked or canned
4 cups vegetable stock
½ cup canned roasted green chilies, chopped

Preparation:
1. Prepare a 12-inch skillet and add the olive oil over medium heat.
2. Add the onion, garlic and green bell pepper. Sauté until slightly tender, approximately 4-5 minutes.
3. Add the tomatillos and cook for an additional 3 minutes, or until softened.
4. Add the collard greens, cumin, chili powder, lime juice, cilantro, and cannellini beans. Toss to mix.
5. Add the vegetable stock and green chilies. Increase heat to medium high and bring chili to a low boil. Reduce heat, cover and simmer for 15- 20 minutes.
6. Transfer ½ of the chili to a blender and pulse until smooth. Add the mixture back into the chili and stir.
7. Serve immediately.

Crisp Green Bean and Egg Hash

Serves: 4-6
Preparation time: 10 minutes
Cooking time: 25 minutes

Ingredients:

½ cup water
2 cups fresh green beans, washed and trimmed
2 tablespoons olive oil
6 cups red potatoes, diced
3 cloves garlic, crushed
1 green bell pepper, diced
1 tablespoon fresh dill, chopped
1 tablespoon fresh chives, chopped
1 teaspoon salt
1 teaspoon black pepper
6 eggs

Preparation:

1. Prepare a 12-inch cast iron skillet and add the water. Heat over medium high and add the green beans. Cook, stirring in the water until bright green, but still crisp. Remove from the pan and set aide, draining any residual water.
2. Add the olive oil to the pan and heat over medium. Add the potatoes, garlic, and bell pepper. Toss to mix.
3. Spread the mixture evenly around the pan, pressing down slightly. Cook for approximately 15 minutes, flipping every 5 minutes, or until potatoes are crisp on the outside.
4. Add the green beans back to the pan and season with dill, chives, salt, and black pepper. Toss lightly.
5. Crack each egg individually over the vegetable hash. Continue to cook for an additional 5 minutes, or until egg whites are set and yolks are desired doneness.

Rosemary Sweet Potato Side

Serves: 6
Preparation time: 10 minutes
Cooking time: 35 minutes

Ingredients:
2 sweet potatoes, peeled
1 onion, sliced
1 red bell pepper, seeded, sliced
½ cup coconut milk
1 teaspoon rosemary
1 teaspoon salt
Extra virgin olive oil

Preparation:
1. Preheat oven to 375 degrees.
2. Slice sweet potatoes into thin rounds (1/4").
3. Heat 2 tablespoons olive oil in cast iron deep skillet, add onions, sauté for a minute, remove pan from heat.
4. Place potato slices around the edges in a circle repeat circles inward, sprinkle with rosemary, salt, and add coconut milk.
5. Cover pan, place in oven for 30 minutes.
6. The Sweet Potato Side works great with any sort of meat or poultry dish or can accompany a tossed salad for a vegetarian meal.

Italian Bean and Tomato Casserole

Serves: 4-6
Preparation time: 10 minutes
Cooking time: 35 minutes

Ingredients:
¼ cup vegetable oil, divided
3 cups day-old French bread, cubed
6 cups heirloom tomatoes, chopped
1 cup sweet yellow onion, diced
4 cloves garlic, crushed and minced
1 tablespoon honey
1 teaspoon salt
1 teaspoon black pepper
3 cups cannellini beans, cooked
3 cups fresh spinach, torn
½ cup fresh basil, chopped
1 tablespoon lemon zest
1 teaspoon crushed red pepper flakes
½ cup parmesan cheese, freshly grated

Preparation:
1. Preheat oven to 350°F.
2. Prepare a 12-inch cast iron skillet and heat the vegetable oil over medium heat. To the pan, add the cubed bread and toss while cooking until the bread cubes are nicely toasted, approximately 5 minutes.
3. Add the tomatoes, onion, and garlic. Season with honey, salt, and black pepper. Cook while stirring for approximately 5 minutes, or until tomatoes begin to soften.
4. Add the cannellini beans, spinach, basil, lemon zest, and crushed red pepper flakes. Toss to mix.
5. Dress the casserole with a drizzle of olive oil and parmesan cheese. Place in the oven and bake for 20-25 minutes.

Pasta and Greens Torte

Servings: 6
Preparation time: 30 minutes
Cooking time: 25 minutes

Ingredients:
1 cup of ricotta cheese
1 pound of fresh Swiss chard
2 cups of cheddar cheese, shredded
1 cup of linguine (1 - 9ounce package)
8 eggs
1 1/2 teaspoons of dried thyme
1/2 teaspoon of pepper
1 1/2 teaspoons of salt
1 cup of milk
3 tablespoons of olive oil

Preparation:
1. Preheat oven to 400°F.
2. Fill a large saucepan with water, and set on the stove. Turn the heat to high.
3. Wash chard, and cut out the stems and ribs. Discard the stems and ribs, and chop the leaves.
4. Cut the linguini in half.
5. Place the chards, and pasta into the boiling water. Cook until the pasta begins to go limp, about 1 to 2 minutes.
6. In a blender, mix the eggs.
7. Add in the milk and ricotta cheese.
8. Season with the thyme, salt, and pepper.
9. Blend until the ingredients are smooth.
10. Coat a 10" cast iron skillet with the olive oil. Place on a stove set to medium.
11. Drain the chard and pasta, and pour into the skillet. You want a fairly even layer of pasta and chard.

12. Shred the cheese and sprinkle over the pasta mixture.
13. Pour the egg mixture over the ingredients. Press the pasta and chard down so it is completely covered by the mixture.
14. Allow it to cook for 2 minutes.
15. Transfer to the oven, and bake for 25 minutes, until the torte is golden brown.
16. Remove from oven, and allow it to sit for 10 minutes.
17. Serve warm.

Potato and Onion Flatbread

Servings: 4
Preparation time: 15 minutes
Cooking time: 20 minutes

Ingredients:

1 yellow onion
1 package of refrigerated pizza dough
1 russet potatoes
1 tablespoon of rosemary needles
1 teaspoon of salt
1/4 teaspoon of black pepper
2 tablespoons of olive oil
2 tablespoons of cornmeal

Preparation:

1. Preheat oven to 450°F.
2. Place a 12" cast iron skillet onto a stove, and set to medium heat.
3. Add the olive oil, and heat thoroughly.
4. Wash, peel, and slice the onions into thin rings.
5. Add to the oil, and cook until they begin to turn golden, about 5 to 7 minutes.
6. Place the onion in a bowl, and remove the skillet from the heat.
7. Wash and slice the potatoes into thin slices. Place in the bowl with the onions.
8. Spice with the salt, pepper and rosemary.
9. Toss the ingredients until the onions and potatoes are coated.
10. Either wipe out the cast iron skillet or use a new one of the same size. Turn it upside down.
11. Roll out the dough until it is roughly the same size as the bottom of the skillet.

12. Dust the bottom of the cast iron skillet with cornmeal.
13. Place the dough on top of the cornmeal.
14. Cover the dough with the potato mixture, making sure that you leave a 1" border around the edge.
15. Place in the oven, and bake until it is golden brown and the potatoes are soft.
16. Remove from oven and serve warm.

Mediterranean Quiche

Serves: 4
Preparation time: 10 minutes
Cooking time: 30 minutes

Ingredients:
8 cups fresh spinach
1 red onion, sliced
2 cloves, garlic
8 eggs
½ cup feta cheese
10 Kalamata olives, pitted, sliced
1 tablespoon flour
2 tablespoons low-fat milk
1 teaspoon salt, black pepper
Extra virgin olive oil

Preparation:
1. Preheat oven to 375 degrees.
2. Heat 3 tablespoons olive oil in cast iron deep skillet over medium-low.
3. Add onion, garlic, sauté for a minute.
4. Add spinach and Kalamata olives, and sauté until spinach wilts.
5. In a bowl, whisk eggs, add milk, salt, pepper, flour, mix, and pour over spinach mixture.
6. Crumble feta cheese on eggs, and place skillet in oven for 20 minutes.
7. Serve quiche with a nice light green salad.

Greek Linguine

Serves: 4
Preparation time: 10 minutes
Cooking time: 15 minutes

Ingredients:
¼ cup + 2 tablespoons olive oil
4 cups tomatoes, chopped
4 cloves garlic, crushed and minced
2 cups spinach, torn
1 teaspoon salt
1 teaspoon black pepper
1 tablespoon lemon juice
½ cup canned artichoke hearts, drained
½ cup Kalamata olives, sliced
1 pound linguine noodles, cooked
1 tablespoon fresh oregano
½ cup fresh parsley, chopped
1 cup feta cheese, crumbled

Preparation:
1. Prepare a 10-inch cast iron skillet and heat 2 tablespoons of olive oil over medium heat. Add the tomatoes and garlic. Sauté until tomatoes begin to break down slightly, 4-5 minutes.
2. Add the spinach and season with salt, black pepper, and lemon juice. Cook for an additional 2 minutes.
3. Add the artichoke hearts, Kalamata olives, and linguine noodles. Toss to mix and heat through.
4. Drizzle the noodles with as much of the remaining olive oil as desired. Season with oregano, parsley, and feta cheese. Toss to mix.
5. Serve immediately while warm.

Hot and Crispy Vegetable Salad

Serves: 4
Preparation time: 15 minutes
Cooking time: 15 minutes

Ingredients:
1 small head cauliflower
4 asparagus spears
2 cups Brussels sprouts
½ cup walnuts
3 eggs, boiled
½ cup water.
1 lemon, juiced
1 teaspoon salt
1 teaspoon black pepper
Extra virgin olive oil

Preparation:
1. Separate cauliflower into florets.
2. Slice asparagus into 1" pieces.
3. Heat 4 tablespoons extra virgin olive oil into cast iron skillet over medium heat.
4. Add asparagus, cauliflower, Brussels sprouts, sauté.
5. Add water, cover, and allow to steam for 10 minutes.
6. Add lemon juice, salt, and black pepper.
7. Slice boiled eggs into 4 wedges.
8. Top salad with boiled eggs, walnuts, and serve.

Cauliflower and Sweet Potato Curry

Serves: 4
Preparation time: 10 minutes
Cooking time: 35 minutes

Ingredients:
1 medium head cauliflower
1 sweet potato
1 carrot, died
1 medium onion, diced
1 medium tomato, diced
4 cloves garlic, minced
1 tablespoon chopped ginger
1 tablespoon organic tomato paste
½ teaspoon cumin seed
½ teaspoon turmeric
1 teaspoon paprika
1 teaspoon black pepper
1 teaspoon salt
¼ cup ghee

Preparation:
1. Peel sweet potato, and slice into 1" pieces.
2. Chop cauliflower into small florets, remove tough skin from cauliflower stem and chop into ½" pieces.
3. Heat ghee, add cumin seeds, toast for 30 seconds.
4. Add onion and garlic, and sauté for a minute, add tomato, ginger, turmeric, and paprika, and cook for 3 minutes.
5. Mix in tomato paste, add sweet potato, carrot, cauliflower, black pepper, salt.
6. Reduce heat to medium low, cover and cook for 30 minutes, or until cauliflower and sweet potato are tender.
7. Serve with Flaxseed tortilla (recipe in Sides and Accompaniments).

Garlic Asparagus Sauté

Serves: 4
Preparation time: 10 min.
Cooking time: 30 minutes

Ingredients:
1 pound asparagus spears
1 red onion, sliced
2 cloves garlic
½ cup cashews, crushed
1 onion, juiced
1 teaspoon salt, black pepper
Extra virgin olive oil

Preparation:
1. Heat 4 tablespoons extra virgin olive oil in skillet.
2. Add onion and garlic, and sauté for a minute.
3. Add asparagus spears, cashew, salt, black pepper, and vegetable stock. Cover and cook on low for 25 minutes or until asparagus is tender.
4. Uncover and allow liquid to evaporate if still remaining.
5. Drizzle with lemon juice before serving.

Veggie Lasagna

Serves: 8
Prep Time: 15 minutes.
Cooking time: 50 minutes

Ingredients:
4 Chinese eggplants
1 green bell pepper, seeded, sliced
1 medium onion, diced
4 cloves garlic
¼ cup Macadamia nuts, chopped
¼ cup cashews, chopped
2 cups pureed tomato
1 lemon, juiced
½ teaspoon black pepper
1 teaspoon salt
Extra virgin olive oil

Preparation:
1. Slice eggplant in half horizontally and in half again vertically, scoop out approximately 1 tablespoon eggplant flesh from each eggplant.
2. Heat 4 tablespoons extra virgin olive oil in cast iron skillet.
3. Add garlic, onion, and bell pepper. Sauté.
4. Add scooped eggplant flesh, sauté for another minute.
5. Pour tomato puree into skillet, mix.
6. Set eggplant in skillet flesh-side up.
7. Spoon tomato puree mixture on top of eggplant, sprinkle with nuts.
8. Cover skillet, and bake in oven for 40 minutes.

Creamy Zucchini Slides

Serves: 8
Preparation time: 5 minutes.
Cooking time: 40 minutes

Ingredients:
4 zucchinis, stemmed
1 red bell pepper, diced
4 cloves garlic, minced
1 can coconut milk
¼ teaspoon horseradish
½ teaspoon paprika
Coconut oil

Preparation:
1. Slice zucchini in half.
2. Heat 4 tablespoons coconut oil in cast iron skillet.
3. Add garlic, bell pepper, and horseradish. Sauté for 1-2 minutes until fragrant.
4. Add zucchini, flesh side down, and brown for a minute, turn over.
5. Pour in coconut milk, sprinkle paprika, salt, and black pepper.
6. Cover skillet, and cook on low for 30 minutes.

ZuCa Noodles

Serves: 4
Preparation time: 10 minutes
Cooking time: 0 minutes

Ingredients:
3 zucchini
1 carrot
½ teaspoon salt
Extra virgin olive oil

Preparation:
1. Peel zucchini and carrot.
2. Use a vegetable peeler, and peel zucchini until you reach seedy center. Save center for another recipe.
3. With the same vegetable peeler, peel carrot wisps.
4. Combine zucchini and carrots with 3 tablespoons extra light olive oil, ½ teaspoon salt.

Cauliflower Flecked with Basil and Pine Nut

Serves: 4
Preparation time: 10 minutes
Cooking time: 10 minutes

Ingredients:
½ medium cauliflower
½ cup medium purple cauliflower
¼ cup pine nuts
¼ cup fresh basil, chopped
½ lemon, juiced
½ kosher salt
½ teaspoon black pepper
2 tablespoons extra virgin olive oil

Preparation:
1. Slice cauliflower into small florets and salt.
2. Heat extra virgin olive oil in a large cast iron skillet over medium-high heat. Add cauliflower, and sauté for 8-10 minutes, until fork tender.
3. Add pine nuts, salt, and black pepper, continue to sauté for another minute.
4. Remove from heat, drizzle with lemon juice, sprinkle with basil, mix, and serve.

Flaxseed Tortilla

Serves: 6
Preparation time: 15 minutes
Cooking time: 5 minutes

Ingredients:
1¼ cup flax meal
1 tablespoon tapioca flour
¼ cup almond milk, warm
¼ teaspoon salt
Extra virgin olive oil

Preparation:
1. Combine flax meal, tapioca flour, and salt, and knead with almond milk.
2. Divide dough into six balls.
3. Place a piece of parchment paper on a flat surface, drop your ball of dough on parchment, and place a second piece of parchment on top.
4. Using rolling pin, roll your flaxseed tortilla.
5. Heat 3 tablespoons olive oil in cast iron skillet.
6. Place flaxseed tortilla in cast iron skillet, cook for 1-1/2 minute per side.

Soups

Ham and Double Cheese Soup

Serves: 4
Preparation time: 20 minutes
Cooking time: 30 minutes

Ingredients:
½ pound ham, cubed
1 potato, diced
1 celery stalk, diced
1 onion, diced
2 tablespoons butter
1 tablespoon flour
1 cup cheddar cheese, shredded
1 cup Swiss cheese, shredded
1 cup milk
2 cups chicken stock
1 cup water
1 teaspoon paprika
1 teaspoon salt, black pepper
Extra virgin olive oil

Preparation:
1. Heat 3 tablespoons extra virgin olive oil in a cast iron deep skillet or Dutch oven, add onion, celery, sauté for 3 minutes.
2. Sauté in ham, and cook for three minutes.
3. Add flour and milk, quickly mix so flour does not become doughy.
4. Add chicken stock, water, salt, black pepper, and paprika, and simmer covered on medium-low for 20 minutes.
5. Reduce heat to low, stir in cheeses.
6. Serve with a slice of good old-fashioned white toast.

Bacon Potato Winter Soup

Serves: 6
Preparation time: 15 minutes
Cooking time: 30 minutes

Ingredients:

5 medium potatoes
½ cup bacon, crumbled
1 sweet onion, diced
4 cups chicken broth
½ cup cream
1 cup milk
1 cup water
2 tablespoons flour
½ teaspoon dry parsley
1 teaspoon each salt, white pepper
Extra virgin olive oil

Topper ingredients:
Sour Cream

Preparation:

1. Slice potatoes into ½" cubes, set aside.
2. Heat 3 tablespoons olive oil in a cast iron deep skillet or Dutch oven.
3. Add sweet onion, sauté until translucent.
4. Mix in flour, slowly pour in chicken stock to form a paste.
5. Mix in remaining liquids, bring potatoes to boil.
6. Add potatoes and bacon, reduce heat to medium, cover, and cook for 25 minutes or until potatoes are tender.
7. Serve with a dollop of sour cream on top.

Portobello Porcini Mushroom Soup

Serves: 4
Preparation time: 15 minutes
Cooking time: 35 minutes

Ingredients:
2 cups Portobello mushrooms, cleaned, quartered
1 cup Porcini mushrooms, chopped
6 cloves garlic, minced
1 medium onion, minced
2 cups low-sodium beef stock
1 cup sour cream
½ teaspoon thyme
½ teaspoon nutmeg
1 teaspoon salt, black pepper
Extra virgin olive oil

Preparation:
1. Heat 3 tablespoons extra virgin olive oil in cast iron deep skillet or Dutch oven, and add onion, garlic. Sauté until fragrant.
2. Add mushrooms, sauté for two minutes, stir in beef stock.
3. Temper sour cream with a little liquid from pan, mix warm sour cream into mushroom mixture.
4. Add spices, reduce heat to low, cover and simmer for 30 minutes.
5. Serve with crusty bread.

Hearty White Bean and Turkey Soup

Serves: 6
Preparation time: 20 minutes
Cooking time: 35 minutes

Ingredients
¾ pound turkey breast, skinless, boneless
1 celery stalk, sliced
¾ cup white beans
1 onion, minced
4 cloves garlic, minced
4 cups low-sodium chicken broth
1 cup water
2 tablespoons tomato paste
1 teaspoon cayenne pepper
1 bay leaf
1 teaspoon salt, black pepper
Extra virgin olive oil

Preparation:
1. Slice chicken breast into 1" cubes.
2. Heat 3 tablespoons extra virgin olive oil in cast iron deep skillet or Dutch oven.
3. Add turkey breast, sauté until browned, remove to dish.
4. Add onion, garlic to cast iron pan, sauté until onion is translucent, mix in tomato paste.
5. Return turkey breast to pan, add remaining ingredients, and bring to boil.
6. Reduce heat to low, cover pot, simmer for 25 minutes.
7. Serve with a slice of hearty Italian bread.

Grandma's Chicken Noodle Soup

Serves: 4
Preparation time: 10 minutes
Cooking time: 25 minutes

Ingredients:
4 cups roasted chicken breast, cubed
1 red onion, diced
3 cloves garlic, minced
1 celery stalk, diced
1 carrot, diced
4 cups low-sodium chicken broth
½ cup dry rotini
1 cup water
½ teaspoon rosemary
½ teaspoon sage
1 teaspoon salt
Extra virgin olive oil

Topping
Handful parsley, chopped

Preparation:
1. Heat 3 tablespoons extra virgin olive oil in a cast iron deep skillet or Dutch oven, add onions, and garlic, and sauté until onion is translucent.
2. Stir in celery stalk, carrot, sauté for a minute.
3. Add chicken broth, water, spices, and bring to boil.
4. Add rotini, cook for 2 minutes.
5. Reduce heat to medium-low, add cubed chicken breast, simmer pot for 20 minutes and serve.
6. Sprinkle with parsley and serve.

Pork and Cabbage Soup

Serves: 4
Preparation time: 20 minutes
Cooking time: 30 minutes

Ingredients:
1 pound pork loin
3 cups cabbage, shredded
4 cups chicken broth
2 cups water
1 potato, diced
1 leek, diced
1 teaspoon rosemary
1 bay leaf
1 teaspoon salt, black pepper
Extra virgin olive oil

Preparation:
1. Slice potatoes into ½" cubes, set aside.
2. Slice pork loin into small cubes, set aside.
3. Heat 3 tablespoons olive oil in a cast iron deep skillet or Dutch oven.
4. Add pork loin, brown.
5. Add cabbage, leek, and sauté for 3 minutes.
6. Mix in potato, rosemary, salt, black pepper.
7. Add chicken broth and water, bring to a boil.
8. Reduce heat, simmer for 20 minutes.
9. Serve with a sourdough bread.

Parmesan Chicken Soup

Serves: 6
Preparation time: 10 minutes
Cooking time: 35 minutes

Ingredients:
4 cups chicken breast, cooked
1 onion, peeled and diced
4 cloves garlic, peeled and minced
2 cups tomato puree
2 cups low-sodium chicken stock
½ cup red wine
¼ cup parsley, chopped
½ cup parmesan, grated
1 teaspoon oregano
1 teaspoon salt, black pepper

Preparation:
1. Heat 3 tablespoons olive oil in a cast iron deep skillet or Dutch oven.
2. Add onion, sauté until translucent.
3. Add chicken breast, sauté for 3 minutes.
4. Stir in tomato puree, red wine, chicken stock, and spices, bring to a boil.
5. Reduce heat to low, simmer for 25 minutes.
6. Stir in parmesan, serve.

Smooth Lentil Carrot Soup

Serves: 6
Preparation time: 10 minutes
Cooking time: 30 minutes

Ingredients:
1 cups red lentils
½ pound carrots, diced
1 sweet onion, minced
3 cloves garlic, minced
1 tablespoon tomato paste
3 cups chicken broth
1 cup water
½ teaspoon oregano
1 teaspoon each salt and black pepper
Extra virgin olive oil

Topping
1 lemon, juiced

Preparation:
1. Heat 3 tablespoons oil in a cast iron deep skillet or Dutch oven over medium heat. Add onion, garlic, sauté until garlic is fragrant.
2. Stir in tomato paste. Add remaining ingredients, bring to boil. Reduce heat, cover, and cook for 25 minutes. Using hand immersion blender, mix until smooth.
3. Add ½ teaspoon of lemon juice per bowl before serving.

Shitake Chicken Soup

Serves: 6
Preparation time: 10 minutes
Cooking time: 45 minutes

Ingredients:
1 pound chicken breasts, skinless, boneless
½ pound shiitake mushrooms
4 cups low-sodium chicken stock
2 tablespoons ginger, grated
2 teaspoons lemongrass, minced
2 carrots, diced
1 onion, peeled, sliced
4 cloves garlic, minced
½ teaspoon salt
1 teaspoon black pepper
1 tablespoon coconut aminos
Extra light olive oil

Preparation:
1. Slice chicken breasts into ½" pieces.
2. Heat 4 tablespoons olive oil in cast iron pot over medium heat, add chicken, brown, and remove chicken breast to plate.
3. Add onions and garlic to same pot, sauté for 30 seconds, add ginger, mushrooms, carrots, lemongrass, and sauté for two minutes.
4. Stir in chicken stock, salt, black pepper, and coconut aminos, cover and simmer for 35 minutes on medium low.

Steak and Broccoli Soup

Serves: 4
Preparation time: 15 minutes
Cooking time: 45 minutes

Ingredients:

1 pound sirloin steak
5 cups broccoli florets
4 cloves garlic, minced
1 medium onion, diced
1 teaspoon coconut flour
1 lemon, juiced
1 teaspoon red pepper flakes
1 teaspoon salt
1 teaspoon black pepper
¼ cup ghee, melted
4 cups low-sodium beef stock
Coconut oil

Preparation:

1. Combine ghee with coconut flour, set aside.
2. Heat 4 tablespoons coconut oil in cast iron pot, add steak and sauté for two minutes.
3. Remove steak from pot.
4. Into same pot, add garlic and onion, sauté for 30 seconds.
5. Add broccoli, continue to sauté for another minute.
6. Return steak to pot, add chicken stock, lemon juice, red pepper, salt, and black pepper. Cover pot, bring to boil, reduce heat to low.
7. Pour 3 tablespoons of liquid from pot, and mix into ghee, add ghee mixture to the pot, and simmer on low for 35 minutes.

Desserts

Most people don't think of desserts when they think of cast iron skillets. However, there are a whole range of desserts that you can make with a cast iron skillet. All of the desserts are delicious proving that the right tool; i.e. the cast iron skillet, can be multifunctional!

Blueberry Peach Pie

Servings: 6
Preparation time: 30 minutes
Cooking time: 40 minutes

Ingredients:
5 cups of blueberries, frozen
2 peaches
1/4 cup of cornstarch
3/4 cup of flour, all purpose
2/3 cup of white sugar
1/2 cup of light brown sugar, firmly packed
1/4 cup of water
2/3 cup of water
1/2 cup of old-fashioned rolled oats
3/4 cup of butter
1 teaspoon of nutmeg
1 lemon

Preparation:
1. Preheat the oven to 400°F.
2. Place a large saucepan on the stove, and set the temperature to medium.
3. Add the blueberries and 1/4 cup of water. Don't thaw the frozen blueberries.

4. Stir in the white sugar.
5. Stirring occasionally, bring the blueberries to a simmer, about 5 minutes.
6. While the blueberries are cooking, whisk together the remaining water and cornstarch in a small bowl. Mix until the cornstarch dissolves.
7. Add the cornstarch to blueberry mixture.
8. Zest the lemon, and add to the blueberries.
9. Wash, peel, and pit the peaches. Slice into 1/2" slices.
10. Add the peaches to the blueberries.
11. Reduce the heat to low, and simmer the fruit until the juices are clear. This will take about 10 to 20 minutes. You want the juice to thicken, and the fruit to be tender.
12. When the mixture is ready, lightly grease a 10" cast iron skillet.
13. Pour the filling into the skillet and set aside.
14. In a separate bowl, mix together the flour and oats.
15. Add in the brown sugar and nutmeg. Mix until the ingredients are blended well.
16. Melt the butter and pour into the dry ingredients.
17. Mix until you have a crumb topping.
18. Sprinkle over the blueberry mixture.
19. Place in the oven and bake for 30 to 40 minutes or until the crumble is golden brown.
20. Remove from the oven.
21. Serve warm.

Lemon Poppy seed Dump Cake

Serves: 8
Prep Time: 5 minutes.
Cooking time: 30 minutes

Ingredients:
1 package lemon pudding mix
1 package Golden Cake mix
¼ cup poppy seeds
1 ½ cup milk
½ cup white chocolate chips
6 ounces butter, melted

Topping ingredients
3 tablespoons poppy seeds for topping

Preparation:
1. Preheat oven to 350 degrees, lightly coat cast iron large skillet with a little butter.
2. In a bowl, combine lemon pudding mix, poppy seeds, Golden cake mix, milk, Golden Cake mix and butter, mix well
3. Pour batter into cast iron skillet, sprinkle with poppy seeds for topping.
4. Bake cake in oven for 30 minutes.

Cherry Clafouti

Servings: 8
Preparation time: 15 minutes
Cooking time: 30 minutes

Ingredients:
2/3 cup of flour, all purpose
6 eggs
1/2 cup of white sugar
1/4 teaspoon of salt
1 tablespoon of butter
1 tablespoon of vanilla
1 1/4 cups of milk
2 tablespoons of brandy
1 1/2 cups of frozen cherries

Preparation:
1. Thaw the frozen cherries.
2. Preheat oven to 400°F.
3. In a large bowl, beat the eggs until they are well blended.
4. Fold in the milk, and mix thoroughly.
5. Whisk in the brandy and vanilla.
6. Add the butter, and mix until the mixture is smooth.
7. In a separate bowl, whisk together the flour and salt.
8. Add to the wet ingredients, and mix until the ingredients are well blended.
9. Grease a 10" cast iron skillet with the butter.
10. Scatter the thawed cherries over the bottom of the skillet.
11. Pour the batter over the cherries.
12. Place in the oven, and bake for 30 minutes or until the pastry is golden brown.
13. Remove from heat.
14. Serve warm.

Caramel Apple Cake

Servings: 8
Preparation time: 20 minutes
Cooking time: 1 hour

Ingredients:
1 cup of light brown sugar, firmly packed
3/4 cup of white sugar
2 cups of flour, all purpose
1/2 cup of chopped pecans
1/2 cup of sour cream
1 tablespoon of lemon juice
2 Granny Smith apples
1/8 teaspoon of nutmeg, ground
3/4 teaspoon of cinnamon, ground
2 teaspoons of vanilla
2 teaspoons of brandy
3/4 cup of milk
1/2 cup of butter
2 eggs

Preparation:
1. Preheat the oven to 350°F.
2. Place the pecans onto a baking sheet, and bake until they are golden, about 8 to 10 minutes.
3. Remove from oven, and allow to cool completely.
4. Increase the oven to 375°F.
5. Wash, peel, and core the apples. Slice into 1/2" thick slices.
6. Place in a bowl with the lemon juice.
7. Add 1 teaspoon of vanilla.
8. Sprinkle in 1/2 teaspoon of cinnamon. Toss until the apples are coated. Set aside.

9. In a 10" cast iron skillet, melt 1/4 cup of butter over a low heat.
10. Remove from heat once the butter is melted, and whisk in the brandy.
11. Add the brown sugar, and mix until it is well blended.
12. Sprinkle the baked pecans over the brown sugar.
13. Arrange the apples over the pecans in an even layer.
14. In a separate bowl, cream together 1/2 cup of white sugar and the remaining 1/4 cup of butter until it is fluffy.
15. Separate the egg whites from the egg yolks. Keep both, but just add the egg yolks, one at a time, to the sugar mixture, blending between each addition.
16. Fold in the sour cream.
17. Add the milk and teaspoon of vanilla. Mix until it is blended. Do not over-mix.
18. In a separate bowl, whisk together the flour, nutmeg, and 1/4 teaspoon of cinnamon.
19. Fold into the wet ingredients. Mix until it is blended. Do not over mix.
20. In a third bowl, whisk the egg whites until they begin to form into soft peaks. Add the 1/4 cup of white sugar, and continue mixing until the peaks form into stiff peaks.
21. Fold into batter.
22. Pour the batter over the apples.
23. Place in the oven, and bake for 50 to 55 minutes or until a toothpick inserted in the center of the cake comes out clean.
24. Remove from heat, cool for 10 minutes in the pan, and then carefully remove from the skillet. The apple and brown sugar should be on top once you tip the cake out of the skillet.
25. Serve warm.

Peach Tart

Servings: 8
Preparation time: 20 minutes
Cooking time: 40 minutes

Ingredients:
8 peaches
1/3 cup of almonds, sliced
1/4 teaspoon of almond extract
2 tablespoons of sugar
3/4 cup of sugar
1 1/2 cups of flour, all purpose
1 1/2 tablespoons of cornstarch
4 tablespoons of ice water
3/4 teaspoon of salt
1 tablespoon of water
1/4 teaspoon of cinnamon, ground
1 egg
1/2 cup of butter, unsalted

Preparation:
1. Preheat the oven to 300°F.
2. Place the almonds on a baking sheet, making sure that they are spread evenly and in a single layer.
3. Bake the almonds for about 15 minutes, or until they are golden brown.
4. Remove from heat, and cool completely.
5. Increase the temperature of the oven to 375°F.
6. Place the cooled almonds into a food processor. Pulse until the almonds are chopped finely.
7. Add in the flour.
8. Add the salt and 1 tablespoon of sugar.
9. Blend until the ingredients are fully mixed.

10. Add the butter and almond extract and again, pulse until you have a dough that resembles oatmeal or small peas.
11. Slowly add the ice water to the mixture, 1 tablespoon at a time, until the dough begins to form around the blades as you pulse. You may not need to use all of the ice water.
12. Remove from the food processor and knead slightly. Form a ball, cover and chill for 30 minutes at least. For the best dough, chill overnight.
13. Wash, peel, pit and slice the peaches. Place in a large bowl.
14. In a separate bowl, whisk together the 3/4 cup of sugar and cornstarch.
15. Fold in the cinnamon.
16. Add to the peaches and toss until the peaches are fully coated.
17. Remove the dough from the fridge and roll out into a 16" circle on a floured surface.
18. Transfer to a 10" cast iron skillet so that the bottom and sides are covered and there is an overhang of dough.
19. Add the peaches to the pie pastry. Create a mound in the middle.
20. Carefully fold the overhanging edges over the top of the peach filling. Be careful not to rip the pastry along the edge of the pan. Also, the pastry will not cover the entire top of the peach filling, there will be a hole in the center.
21. Beat the egg and tablespoon of water in a small bowl.
22. Brush over the pastry.
23. Sprinkle with the 1 tablespoon of sugar.
24. Place in the oven, and bake for 35 to 40 minutes or until golden brown.
25. Remove from oven, and let stand for an hour before serving.
26. Serve warm or cold.

Maple Vanilla Custard

Serves: 6
Preparation time: 10 minutes
Cooking time: 10 minutes

Ingredients:
4 eggs
4 cups milk
1 teaspoon vanilla bean, crushed
½ cup maple syrup
½ teaspoon salt
Butter

Preparation:
1. Whisk eggs in bowl, mix in vanilla, maple syrup, and salt.
2. Pour milk into cast iron pot, bring to simmer.
3. Remove milk from stove.
4. Add a tablespoon at a time of hot milk into egg mixture, mixing continuously in order not to cook egg.
5. Once egg mixture has been tempered with milk, whisk egg mixture into pot of milk.
6. Return pot to stove, and simmer for 5 minutes.
7. Cool and serve.

Fruit N Cream Crêpes

Serves: 12
Preparation time: 15 minutes
Cooking time: 25 minutes

Ingredients:
3 cups almond flour
2 teaspoons flax meal
2 eggs
2 tablespoons water
½ teaspoon salt
Almond oil

Filling ingredients
Fresh berries, peaches
Whipped Cream

Preparation:
1. Whisk eggs, and gradually add in almond flour, mix.
2. Add 1 teaspoon almond oil, salt, flax meal, water, and continue mixing until smooth.
3. Heat 2 tablespoons almond oil in 10" cast iron skillet, spoon 3 tablespoons mixture into skillet.
4. Cook for a minute per side.
5. Stuff with fruits and whipped cream, serve.

Cookie in a Pan

Servings: 16 small slices
Preparation time: 15 minutes
Cooking time: 30 minutes

Ingredients:
2 1/2 cups of flour, all purpose
1 cup of light brown sugar, firmly packed
1/2 cup of white sugar
1 teaspoon of baking soda
1 teaspoon of salt
1 teaspoon of vanilla
1 cup of butter, unsalted
2 cups of chocolate chips
2 eggs

Preparation:
1. Preheat the oven to 375°F.
2. In a large bowl, cream together the butter, white sugar, and brown sugar until you have a smooth mixture.
3. Fold in the vanilla, and mix well.
4. Add the first egg, and mix until it is incorporated.
5. Add the second egg, and mix the ingredients until the batter is smooth.
6. In a separate bowl, whisk together the flour, salt and baking soda.
7. Fold into the wet ingredients, and mix until you have a stiff dough.
8. Mix in the chocolate chips.
9. Lightly grease a 10" cast iron skillet.

10. Turn the dough into the skillet, and press evenly around the skillet so you have a thick, even layer of cookie dough. At this point, you can decorate the top of the cookie with M&M's, nuts, Smarties, or sprinkles, or you can just leave it plain.
11. Place in the oven, and bake for about 20 minutes until the edges of the cookie are lightly browned.
12. Remove from the oven, and carefully remove from the skillet.
13. Cool for 15 minutes before serving.

Raspberry White Chocolate Dump Cake

Serves: 8
Preparation time: 5 minutes.
Cooking time: 35 minutes

Ingredients:
1 package raspberry pudding mix
1 package Angel Food Cake mix
1 ½ cup milk
½ cup white chocolate chips
6 ounces butter, melted

Preparation:
1. Preheat oven to 350 degrees, lightly coat cast iron large skillet with a little butter.
2. In a bowl, combine milk, raspberry pudding mix, Angel Food Cake mix, and white chocolate chips.
3. Pour batter into cast iron skillet, drizzle with butter, and place in oven for 35 minutes.

Apple Caramel Cake

Serves: 8
Prep Time: 15 minutes.
Cooking time: 25 minutes

Ingredients:

2 medium-sized Gala apples, peeled, cored
½ cup walnuts
½ cup caramel candies
1 cup all-purpose flour
½ cup brown sugar
3 eggs
2 teaspoons baking powder
½ teaspoon vanilla
½ teaspoon ground cinnamon
¼ teaspoon ground cloves
¼ teaspoon salt
Coconut oil

Preparation:

1. Preheat oven to 350 degrees, coat a 10" cast iron skillet with a little coconut oil
2. Thinly-slice half an apple for topping, dice remaining apple.
3. Place 1/3 cup coconut oil and brown sugar in food processor, mix.
4. Add eggs to butter mixture and beat.
5. Sift flour and combine with cinnamon, cloves, salt and baking powder.
6. Slowly add dry ingredients to food processor, continue mixing.
7. Add vanilla, walnuts, caramel candies, mix.
8. Pour mixture into cast iron skillet, top with apple slices and place in oven for 25 minutes.

Apple Pie

Servings: 8
Preparation time: 20 minutes
Cooking time: 1 hour and 50 minutes

Ingredients:
2 pounds of Granny Smith apples (about 10)
2 pounds of Braeburn apples (about 10)
2 tablespoons of white sugar
3/4 cup of white sugar
1 cup of light brown sugar, firmly packed
1 teaspoon of ground cinnamon
1/2 cup of butter
1 egg
2 premade pie crusts

Preparation:
1. Preheat the oven to 350°F.
2. Wash, peel, and core apples. Slice them into 1/2" slices.
3. Place the apples in a bowl.
4. Add the cinnamon and 3/4 cup of white sugar. Toss until the apples are coated.
5. Place a 10" cast iron skillet onto the stove. Set heat to medium.
6. Melt the butter in the pan.
7. Add the brown sugar, and cook for about 2 minutes. Stir constantly and cook until the sugar is dissolved.
8. Remove the skillet from the heat, and spread out the brown sugar mixture so that it coats the bottom of the skillet.
9. Remove the premade pie crust from its metal pan. Place the piecrust on top of the brown sugar.
10. Pour the apple mixture into the pie crust.

11. Top with the second pie crust, remembering to remove it from the pan it is packaged in. Crimp the edges of the two piecrusts with your fingers.
12. Separate the egg yolk and the egg white. Throw away the egg yolk, and brush the egg white over the top of the pie crust.
13. Make 4 to 5 slits on the top of the pie for venting.
14. Place in the oven for an 60 to 70 minutes. You want the pie to be golden brown and the filling to be bubbling.
15. Remove from the oven, and cool for 30 minutes before serving.
16. Serve warm or cold.

Chocolate Chip Dutch Baby

Servings: 6
Preparation time: 10 minutes
Cooking time: 15 minutes

Ingredients:

1/2 cup of flour
3 bananas
3/4 cup of milk
1/2 cup of coffee-flavored liqueur
2 tablespoons of butter
2 tablespoons of sugar
1/4 teaspoon of salt
1/3 cup of chocolate chips, semi sweet
1/2 cup of whipped topping
2 eggs

Preparation:

1. Preheat oven to 450°F.
2. Place a 9" cast iron skillet in the oven to heat. This should take about 15 minutes.
3. In a large bowl, whisk together the flour, sugar and salt.
4. Pour in the milk, and mix well.
5. Add the first egg, and mix until it is incorporated.
6. Add the second egg, and mix the ingredients until the batter is smooth.
7. Remove the skillet from the oven, and add 1 tablespoon of butter. Melt it, and swirl it around the skillet until the skillet is evenly coated. It is okay if the butter goes brown as it will add flavor to the dish. If it does not melt and go brown, return it to the oven for 2 to 3 minutes until the butter is browned.
8. Pour the batter into the hot cast iron skillet.
9. Sprinkle the chocolate chips evenly around the batter.

10. Return the skillet to the oven, and bake until the pastry is puffed and golden brown, about 10 minutes.
11. Remove from the oven.
12. Cut the bananas lengthwise.
13. Place a second cast iron skillet onto the stove and set the heat to medium-high.
14. Melt the remaining tablespoon of butter.
15. Add the bananas, and cook until they are brown. This usually takes 2 minutes on each side.
16. Pour in the liqueur, and simmer for 1 minutes.
17. Remove from heat.
18. Top the pastry with the banana mixture.
19. Garnish with whipped topping and serve warm.

Mini Berry Cobbler

Servings: 6
Preparation time: 15 minutes
Cooking time: 25 minutes

Ingredients:

4 cups of mixed berries, frozen mixture
1 tablespoon of cornstarch
1 1/2 cups of flour, all purpose
2/3 cups of butter
2 tablespoons of butter
1/3 cup of white sugar
1/4 cup of white sugar
1/2 teaspoon of salt
2 teaspoons of baking powder
1/2 cup of buttermilk
3 tablespoons of crystallized ginger

Preparation:

1. Preheat the oven to 400°F.
2. Place the mixed berries into a large bowl.
3. Melt the 2 tablespoons of butter. Pour it over the berries.
4. Add the 1/4 cup of sugar and the cornstarch. Toss until the berries are coated. Set aside.
5. In a separate bowl, whisk together the flour and the 1/3 cup of sugar.
6. Add the crystallized ginger.
7. Stir in the baking powder and salt. Mix until the ingredients are blended well.
8. At the 2/3 cups of butter, and cut into the flour with a pastry knife. Mix until you have a crumbly mixture.
9. Slowly add the buttermilk, and mix until you have a soft dough.

10. Turn the dough out onto a floured surface. Knead it 3 to 4 times.
11. Pat into a 6"x4" rectangle that is about 1" thick.
12. Cut the dough into 6 squares, and then cut the squares into 12 triangles.
13. Grease 6 4" cast iron skillets.
14. Place 1 triangle of dough in each of the 6 skillets.
15. Top with the berry mixture. Make it even amounts in each skillet.
16. Place a second triangle of dough over each berry topping.
17. Place in the oven for 20 to 24 minutes, or until the pastry is golden brown and the fruit is bubbling.
18. Remove from heat, and cool for 15 minutes.
19. Serve warm.

Cinnamon Raisin Nut Dump Cake

Serves: 8
Prep Time: 5 minutes.
Cooking time: 20 minutes

Ingredients:
1 package Spice Cake mix
2 cups milk
½ cup raisins
¼ cup walnuts
½ teaspoon cinnamon
Butter

Preparation:
1. Preheat oven to 350 degrees and coat cast iron large skillet with a little butter.
2. Mix remaining ingredients in bowl, and pour into a large cast iron skillet. Place in oven for 20 minutes.

Walnut Apple Crumble

Serves: 6
Preparation time: 15 minutes
Cooking time: 35 minutes

Ingredients
5 Granny Smith apples, peeled, cored, diced
½ cup walnuts, crushed
½ cup brown sugar
¾ cup all-purpose flour
½ cup rolled oats
1 teaspoon cinnamon
1 cup butter

Topping ingredients (optional)
Vanilla Ice Cream

Preparation:
1. Preheat oven to 350 degrees.
2. Place ¼ cup butter in cast iron deep skillet, melt over medium heat.
3. Add apples, walnuts, and ½ teaspoon cinnamon to skillet,
4. Continue to stir until apples are soft and 80 percent of water has dissipated, approximately 12 minutes.
5. In separate bowl, combine brown sugar, flour, rolled oats, ½ teaspoon cinnamon and remaining butter.
6. Crumble mixture with fork.
7. Sprinkle crumbs over apples, and stick into oven for 20 minutes.
8. Serve with creamy vanilla ice cream.

Conclusion

Cast iron cookware makes whipping up a full three-course meal a snap, even during weekdays. The recipes provided in this book give you a chance to sample a variety of dishes from the traditional to those with ethnic influences. The diversity also gives you a chance to check out the numerous ways you can use cast iron in the kitchen.

If you've had a chance to try out the dishes, we hope you enjoyed them and are inspired to whip up a few of your own as well. If you have yet to start creating, then rest assured you are in for a treat of the fabulous taste sensation kind.

We hope this meal collection will bring you ease of cooking and provide you with more time to spend with your family - that's what it's all about.

Happy cast iron cooking!

More Books by Marie Adams

Appendix – Cooking Conversion Charts

1. Measuring Equivalent Chart

Type	Imperial	Imperial	Metric
Weight	1 dry ounce		28g
	1 pound	16 dry ounces	0.45 kg
Volume	1 teaspoon		5 ml
	1 dessert spoon	2 teaspoons	10 ml
	1 tablespoon	3 teaspoons	15 ml
	1 Australian tablespoon	4 teaspoons	20 ml
	1 fluid ounce	2 tablespoons	30 ml
	1 cup	16 tablespoons	240 ml
	1 cup	8 fluid ounces	240 ml
	1 pint	2 cups	470 ml
	1 quart	2 pints	0.95 l
	1 gallon	4 quarts	3.8 l
Length	1 inch		2.54 cm

*   Numbers are rounded to the closest equivalent

2. Oven Temperature Equivalent Chart

T(°F)	T(°C)
220	100
225	110
250	120
275	140
300	150
325	160
350	180
375	190
400	200
425	220
450	230
475	250
500	260

* $T(°C) = [T(°F)-32] * 5/9$

** $T(°F) = T(°C) * 9/5 + 32$

*** Numbers are rounded to the closest equivalent

62605041R00137

Made in the USA
Lexington, KY
12 April 2017